Level UP
Your ACT® Math Score

Michelle Burrier
Matthew Deevers
Cristina González Alcalá
Laura Magni
David Opfer

Summit
Education
Initiative ™

i

Cameron Tucker

Level UP your ACT® Math Score

Developed by Summit Education Initiative

FIRST EDITION

ISBN: 978-0-9978068-0-9

Library of Congress Control Number: 2016947110

ACT is a registered trademark of ACT, Inc., which was not involved in the production of, and does not endorse, this book.

Published by Summit Education Initiative
120 E. Mill Street, Suite 330
Akron, Ohio 44308
www.seisummit.org

Acknowledgments

Funding and support for this project came from Lumina™ Foundation and the GAR Foundation. We thank Lumina™ for their national leadership in postsecondary readiness and degree completion. We thank GAR for their ongoing, passionate promotion of quality of life, education and economic opportunities for students and residents of Akron, Ohio and Summit County.

We would like to thank the Summit County Ready High School Network members for their initial feedback on the concepts for the course and book.

David Opfer and Laura Magni provided the content for this book and the accompanying course as contract professionals. They also beta-tested the course in the spring of 2015 as volunteers. Without their work and dedication to quality, we would not be where we are today.

We thank Mona Kotran of Akron Early College High School and Akron Public Schools for piloting the course and providing feedback. Ms. Kotran's commitment to students and attention to detail helped us identify ways to make this book better. Additionally, we benefitted from the support and feedback of C. Michael Neag, whose observations during the pilot program provided additional insight. Mike's ongoing support for this work has motivated us to keep moving forward for several years.

David Toth provided the initial inspiration for the formatting of this book. David was the first to help us visualize our work as a final product.

Michelle Burrier has turned our vision into a reality that exceeded expectations. Michelle's work and patience have been key to our success.

- Summit Education Initiative, 2016

This page intentionally left blank

Table of Contents

This page intentionally left blank

Introduction

How to Use this Book

Congratulations! You have decided to prepare yourself for the ACT® Math test using the best method in the world: practice! **Success on the ACT® comes down to effort and strategy**. This book can help you with both. Use the videos to learn the best strategies. Complete all the practice problems, quizzes and tests and you will have put in the effort.

This book is designed to accompany the *Level UP Your ACT® Math Score* course. If you are using this book because you are enrolled in a *Level UP* course, follow along with your instructor. The course is designed to show you examples, and to pace you through practice problems, quizzes and homework assignments.

Use the videos!

If you are not enrolled in a *Level UP* course, you can work your way through the book on your own. Access all the instructional videos by scanning the QR codes in the book. If you don't have a QR code scanner, you can find playlists of videos at the Summit Education Initiative channel on YouTube® (www.youtube.com/user/SEISummit).

The ACT® Math test has three levels of difficulty: Novice (pre-algebra and elementary algebra); Intermediate (intermediate algebra and coordinate geometry); and Advanced (plane geometry and trigonometry). This book follows that same format. There are three classes in the novice course, three classes in the intermediate course and two classes in the advanced course. Each class has quizzes (to be taken during class) and homework assignments (to be completed after class). When you finish all the work, you will have completed over 300 practice problems!

Use the practice tests to measure your growth

This book also has two full-length practice Math tests. Take the pre-test *before* you start any practice. Then take the post-test at the end of the Advanced course to see how much you have improved.

Details of this book

The ACT® Math test is like a race. It's a race between you and the test. During the Math test, you will have 60 minutes to answer 60 questions. If you are going to Level UP, you need to train yourself to answer questions quickly, using the best strategies you have.

Tidbits and Takes

Most of the questions you see in this book are *Tidbit* questions or *Take* questions. When you see a *Tidbit* question, try to answer it on your own in ONE MINUTE OR LESS. Then watch the video to see how a teacher would solve the problem. When you see a *Take* question, try to answer it in the specific number of seconds you're given. For example, if you see a *Take 45* question, try to answer it in 45 seconds. If you see a *Take 70* question, you have 70 seconds to solve it. If you want to see how a Take problem was solved, go back and watch the video at the end of a class. Sticking to these time limits will train you to finish the ACT® Math test in the right amount of time.

Self-Assessment Zones

There are many self-assessment zones in this book. Use these to track your own understanding, and to remind yourself to review a specific problem. An example Self-Assessment Zone is completed below. Notice how the student got the right answer, but realized it was a lucky guess. By circling the QR code, this student has set a reminder to go back and review the video solution later. The most successful people in the world are the ones who always think about how they're doing, and who have a plan to improve.

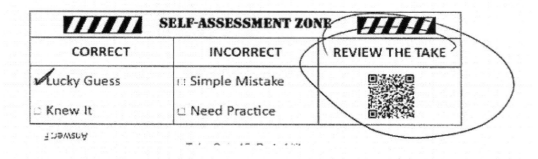

Understanding the Book's Numbering System

The *Tidbits*, *Takes* and Homework problems are all labeled with a 3-digit code. The first number is the course number, the second number is the class number and the third number is the problem number. For example, **Tidbit 2.1.7** is a problem you would see in Course 2, Class 1; it would be the 7th *Tidbit* problem in that class.

Setting a Good Pace on Quizzes and Homework Assignments

Quizzes are all timed for one minute per question and will be taken in class. If you are using this book on your own, set a timer so that the number of minutes you have equals the number of questions on the quiz. If there are 7 questions on a quiz, try to complete the quiz in about 7 minutes. ***This is especially important in Course 1***. Learn to answer the pre-algebra and basic algebra questions quickly so that you can "bank" time for the harder questions at the end.

Try to complete all your homework assignments in 10 minutes. There are two different types of homework problems. The "Day After" homework should be completed the day after class, while everything is fresh in your mind. The "So I don't forget" assignment should be completed a few days before the next class, just as a refresher *so you don't forget.* If you get stuck on a homework assignment, you can watch a video to see how all the problems were solved.

Do yourself a favor: SET A GOAL

Before you begin, think about why you're practicing in the first place. What do you hope to get out of this? What will a higher ACT® Math score mean to you? How will a better score help you get something else that's important to you? Will this score help you meet the NCAA Clearinghouse requirement? Will it help you get into college-level courses right away? Are you trying to raise your score so that you can get into a more selective college, or so you can earn a scholarship?

Think about this and then write down a goal in the space below. There will be times during this course when your motivation is low. This goal can help you keep going.

My Goal:

_____

_____

_____

_____

Other Resources

For more practice visit **www.actstudent.org**. There are many free resources on the ACT® site. You can find additional free practice questions, learn more about the test format, get a free study guide, or sign up for a free ACT® question of the day. There are also resources on the ACT® site that are not free. Ask a school counselor, your math teacher or another adult before paying for any resources or materials.

Remember, all the *Take, Tidbit* and homework questions can be found at:

www.youtube.com/user/SEISummit

ACT® Math Facts

There are 60 questions to be completed in 60 minutes. The ACT® test is a race. This course will train you to complete questions better and faster. Each class has a fast pace so if you don't get an answer mark it for later to review.

Calculators are permitted, however, they should be used strategically to save time. If you take a calculator, you should check the regulations on www.actstudent.org to make sure your calculator is not prohibited. Use of a prohibited calculator could result in you being dismissed from the test. Finally, if your calculator uses batteries make sure you bring an extra set of batteries.

The ACT® Math test covers the following topics:

Topic	Average Questions	Percent of the Test
Pre-Algebra	12 – 15	35% - 45%
Elementary Algebra	9 – 12	
Intermediate Algebra	9 – 12	30% - 40%
Coordinate Geometry	9 – 12	
Plane Geometry	12 – 15	25% - 35%
Trigonometry	3 – 6	

Here is some ACT® Math trivia for you:

- Almost HALF the questions you see on the test were taught in 8th or 9th grade, so you may need to go back and review a few skills.
- The ACT® will usually have "distractor" answers as choices. Be sure to read each question carefully so you know what is being asked.
- You will NEVER see more than 6 trigonometry questions on an ACT® Math test
- There is no "I" answer option on the ACT® test. The letter "I" looks too much like the number 1, so they don't use it. Your answer choices are A B C D E or F G H J K.
- An average high school student in the United States in 2015 correctly answered about HALF the questions on the Math section.
- Students who correctly answer 40 questions (out of 60) are in the TOP 25% of all high school students in the United States.
- Most experts agree that a 22 on the Math section of the ACT® is a "college-ready" score. To earn a score of 22, you need to answer about 33 questions correctly.

This page intentionally left blank

We all START somewhere.
This is where YOU are NOW.

Every step

gets you closer to

SUCCESS

This page intentionally left blank

Course Material

This page intentionally left blank

Novice Course

Class one

- Inequalities and Equations
- Polynomials

This page intentionally left blank

Inequalities and Equations (Simple Inequalities)

Which of the following is equivalent to the inequality $3x - 11 < x + 7$?
- A. $x < -9$
- B. $x < -2$
- C. $x > -2$
- D. $x < 9$
- E. $x > 9$

Notes:

///// SELF-ASSESSMENT ZONE /////		
CORRECT	**INCORRECT**	**REVIEW THE TIDBIT**
☐ Lucky Guess	☐ Simple Mistake	
☐ Knew It	☐ Need Practice	

Do not turn the page until you are ready to proceed with the timed TAKE problem

STOP

Inequalities and Equations (Simple Inequalities)

Take 40

Which of the following is equivalent to the inequality $5x + 14 > -2x - 7$?

  A. $x > -7$
  B. $x < -3$
  C. $x > -3$
  D. $x < 1$
  E. $x > 1$

▨▨▨▨ SELF-ASSESSMENT ZONE ▨▨▨▨		
CORRECT	**INCORRECT**	**REVIEW THE TAKE**
☐ Lucky Guess	☐ Simple Mistake	
☐ Knew It	☐ Need Practice	

Answer: C

Inequalities and Equations (Complex Inequalities)

Which of the following is equivalent to the inequality $2x + 13 < 5x - 20$?

    F. $x > -11$

    G. $x < \dfrac{7}{3}$

    H. $x > \dfrac{7}{3}$

    J. $x < 11$

    K. $x > 11$

Notes:

/////// SELF-ASSESSMENT ZONE ///////		
CORRECT	**INCORRECT**	**REVIEW THE TIDBIT**
☐ Lucky Guess	☐ Simple Mistake	
☐ Knew It	☐ Need Practice	

Do not turn the page until you are ready to proceed with the timed TAKE problem

Inequalities and Equations (Complex Inequalities)

Take 40

Which of the following is equivalent to the inequality $3x + 2 > 4x - 3$?

    F. $x < -5$
    G. $x > -5$
    H. $x < 1$
    J. $x < 5$
    K. $x > 5$

⬛⬛⬛ SELF-ASSESSMENT ZONE ⬛⬛⬛		
CORRECT	**INCORRECT**	**REVIEW THE TAKE**
☐ Lucky Guess	☐ Simple Mistake	
☐ Knew It	☐ Need Practice	

Answer: J

Inequalities and Equations (Inequality with Distribution)

Which of the following is equivalent to the inequality $-3(x + 2) > 4(2x - 1)$?

A. $x < -\dfrac{2}{11}$

B. $x > -\dfrac{2}{11}$

C. $x < -\dfrac{11}{2}$

D. $x > -\dfrac{11}{2}$

E. $x < \dfrac{5}{11}$

Notes:

▨▨ SELF-ASSESSMENT ZONE ▨▨		
CORRECT	**INCORRECT**	**REVIEW THE TIDBIT**
☐ Lucky Guess	☐ Simple Mistake	
☐ Knew It	☐ Need Practice	

Do not turn the page until you are ready to proceed with the timed TAKE problem

STOP

Inequalities and Equations (Inequality with Distribution)

Take 45

Which of the following is equivalent to the inequality $2(2x - 7) > 2(x - 5)$?

    A. $x > -12$
    B. $x < 1$
    C. $x > 1$
    D. $x < 2$
    E. $x > 2$

▰▰▰▰ SELF-ASSESSMENT ZONE ▰▰▰▰		
CORRECT	**INCORRECT**	**REVIEW THE TAKE**
□ Lucky Guess	□ Simple Mistake	
□ Knew It	□ Need Practice	

Answer: E

Inequalities and Equations (Simple Equation)

If $3x + 5 = 14$, then $2x =$?

    F.   3
    G.   6
    H. $\frac{19}{3}$
    J.   9
    K.   27

Notes:

////// SELF-ASSESSMENT ZONE //////		
CORRECT	**INCORRECT**	**REVIEW THE TIDBIT**
☐ Lucky Guess	☐ Simple Mistake	
☐ Knew It	☐ Need Practice	

Do not turn the page until you are ready to proceed with the timed TAKE problem

Inequalities and Equations (Simple Equation)

Take 35

If $2x - 11 = -19$, then $2x =$?

    F. -30

    G. -16

    H. -15

    J. -8

    K. -4

///// SELF-ASSESSMENT ZONE /////		
CORRECT	**INCORRECT**	**REVIEW THE TAKE**
□ Lucky Guess	□ Simple Mistake	
□ Knew It	□ Need Practice	

Answer: J

Inequalities and Equations (Absolute Value)

-2|3 − 7| =?

    A. −20

    B. −8

    C. 2

    D. 8

    E. 20

Notes:

▨▨▨▨ SELF-ASSESSMENT ZONE ▨▨▨▨		
CORRECT	**INCORRECT**	**REVIEW THE TIDBIT**
☐ Lucky Guess	☐ Simple Mistake	
☐ Knew It	☐ Need Practice	

Do not turn the page until you are ready to proceed with the timed TAKE problem

Inequalities and Equations (Absolute Value)

Take 30

$|4 - 6| - |20 - 3|$?

A. -19
B. -15
C. 2
D. 15
E. 19

〃〃〃 SELF-ASSESSMENT ZONE 〃〃〃		
CORRECT	**INCORRECT**	**REVIEW THE TAKE**
□ Lucky Guess	□ Simple Mistake	
□ Knew It	□ Need Practice	

Answer: B

Take Quiz 1: Inequalities and Equations

Page 160

14

Polynomials (Subtracting Polynomials)

The expression $(3x - 1) - (2x - 3)$ is equivalent to:

    A. $6x^2 + 3$
    B. $6x^2 - 11x + 3$
    C. $5x - 4$
    D. $x + 2$
    E. $x - 4$

Notes:

/////// SELF-ASSESSMENT ZONE ///////		
CORRECT	**INCORRECT**	**REVIEW THE TIDBIT**
☐ Lucky Guess	☐ Simple Mistake	
☐ Knew It	☐ Need Practice	

Do not turn the page until you are ready to proceed with the timed TAKE problem

Polynomials (Subtracting Polynomials)

Take 45

The expression $(6t + 4) - (-t - 1)$ is equivalent to:

    A. $7t + 5$
    B. $7t + 3$
    C. $5t + 3$
    D. $-6t^2 - 10t - 4$
    E. $-6t^2 - 4$

▨▨▨ SELF-ASSESSMENT ZONE ▨▨▨		
CORRECT	**INCORRECT**	**REVIEW THE TAKE**
□ Lucky Guess	□ Simple Mistake	
□ Knew It	□ Need Practice	

Answer: A

Polynomials (Multiplying Monomials)

The product $(3x^7y^2)(4x^5y)$ is equivalent to:

F. $12x^{35}y^2$
G. $12x^{12}y^3$
H. $12x^{12}y^2$
J. $7x^{35}y^2$
K. $7x^{12}y^3$

Notes:

///// SELF-ASSESSMENT ZONE /////		
CORRECT	**INCORRECT**	**REVIEW THE TIDBIT**
☐ Lucky Guess	☐ Simple Mistake	
☐ Knew It	☐ Need Practice	

Do not turn the page until you are ready to proceed with the timed TAKE problem

Polynomials (Multiplying Monomials)

Take 30

The product $(2x^3y^4)(3x^7y^2)$ is equivalent to:

F. $6x^{21}y^8$
G. $6x^{10}y^6$
H. $5x^{21}y^8$
J. $5x^{10}y^6$
K. x^4y^2

///// SELF-ASSESSMENT ZONE /////		
CORRECT	**INCORRECT**	**REVIEW THE TAKE**
□ Lucky Guess	□ Simple Mistake	
□ Knew It	□ Need Practice	

Answer: G

Polynomials (Multiplying Binomials)

The expression $(4x - 5y^2)(4x + 5y^2)$ is equivalent to:

    A. $16x^2 - 25y^4$
    B. $16x^2 - 10y^4$
    C. $16x^2 + 25y^4$
    D. $8x^2 - 25y^4$
    E. $8x^2 - 10y^4$

Notes:

▨ **SELF-ASSESSMENT ZONE** ▨		
CORRECT	**INCORRECT**	**REVIEW THE TIDBIT**
□ Lucky Guess	□ Simple Mistake	
□ Knew It	□ Need Practice	

Do not turn the page until you are ready to proceed with the timed TAKE problem

Polynomials (Multiplying Binomials)

Take 50

The expression $(7x + 3y^2)(7x - 3y^2)$ is equivalent to:

    A. $49x^2 - 9y^4$
    B. $49x^2 - 6y^4$
    C. $49x^2 - 9y^4$
    D. $14x^2 - 9y^4$
    E. $14x^2 - 6y^4$

▨▨▨▨ SELF-ASSESSMENT ZONE ▨▨▨▨		
CORRECT	**INCORRECT**	**REVIEW THE TAKE**
☐ Lucky Guess	☐ Simple Mistake	
☐ Knew It	☐ Need Practice	

Answer: A

Polynomials (Squaring a Binomial)

For all X, $(5x - 3)^2 = ?$

    F. $10x - 6$
    G. $10x^2 - 6$
    H. $25x^2 + 9$
    J. $25x^2 - 15x + 9$
    K. $25x^2 - 30x + 9$

Notes:

▨▨▨ SELF-ASSESSMENT ZONE ▨▨▨		
CORRECT	**INCORRECT**	**REVIEW THE TIDBIT**
□ Lucky Guess	□ Simple Mistake	
□ Knew It	□ Need Practice	

Do not turn the page until you are ready to proceed with the timed TAKE problem

Polynomials (Squaring a Binomial)

Take 45

For all , $(2x + 7)^2 = ?$

     F. $4x + 14$

     G. $4x^2 + 14$

     H. $4x^2 + 49$

     J. $4x^2 + 14x + 49$

     K. $4x^2 + 28x + 49$

 SELF-ASSESSMENT ZONE 		
CORRECT	**INCORRECT**	**REVIEW THE TAKE**
□ Lucky Guess	□ Simple Mistake	
□ Knew It	□ Need Practice	

Answer: K   Take Quiz 2: Polynomials

Page 164

Congratulations!

You completed the novice course, class one!

There is a difference between not knowing and not knowing yet.

— Shelia Tobias

Novice Course

Class two

- Proportions
- Percentages
- Averages
- Median and Mode

Proportions (Cross Multiply)

At your sales job, you find the amount you earn in commission is directly proportional to how many hours you work per week. Last week you earned $422 working 25 hours. About how much will you earn in commission this week if you work 28 hours?

   A. $480
   B. $472
   C. $421
   D. $377
   E. $250

Notes:

 SELF-ASSESSMENT ZONE 		
CORRECT	**INCORRECT**	**REVIEW THE TIDBIT**
□ Lucky Guess	□ Simple Mistake	
□ Knew It	□ Need Practice	

Do not turn the page until you are ready to proceed with the timed TAKE problem

Proportions (Cross Multiply)

Take 40

If a house appeared 5 inches tall on a 32" flat screen, how tall will that same house appear on a similar 52" flat screen?

    A. 332.8"
    B. 57"
    C. 25"
    D. 8.125"
    E. 3.1"

SELF-ASSESSMENT ZONE		
CORRECT	**INCORRECT**	**REVIEW THE TAKE**
☐ Lucky Guess	☐ Simple Mistake	
☐ Knew It	☐ Need Practice	

Answer: D

Percentages (Sales Price)

A shirt that originally costs $34.99 is on sale for 15% off. What is the sale price of the shirt before tax?

    A. $5.25
    B. $17.49
    C. $19.99
    D. $29.74
    E. $40.24

Notes:

////// SELF-ASSESSMENT ZONE //////		
CORRECT	**INCORRECT**	**REVIEW THE TIDBIT**
☐ Lucky Guess	☐ Simple Mistake	
☐ Knew It	☐ Need Practice	

Do not turn the page until you are ready to proceed with the timed TAKE problem

Percentages (Sales Price)

Take 50

At the bookstore, best-sellers are normally $19.95 each. During the store-wide 20% off sale, how much would it cost you, before tax, to buy two best-sellers?

    F. $3.99
    G. $7.98
    H. $15.96
    J. $31.92
    K. $39.90

▨▨▨▨ SELF-ASSESSMENT ZONE ▨▨▨▨		
CORRECT	**INCORRECT**	**REVIEW THE TAKE**
□ Lucky Guess	□ Simple Mistake	
□ Knew It	□ Need Practice	

Answer: J

Percentages (Decreasing)

A number is decreased by 40% and the result is 54. What is the number?
- A. 94
- B. 90
- C. 75.6
- D. 21.6
- E. 14

Notes:

SELF-ASSESSMENT ZONE		
CORRECT	**INCORRECT**	**REVIEW THE TIDBIT**
□ Lucky Guess	□ Simple Mistake	
□ Knew It	□ Need Practice	

Do not turn the page until you are ready to proceed with the timed TAKE problem

Percentages (Decreasing)

Take 50

A number is decreased by 30% and the result is 77. What is the number?

    A. 110
    B. 107
    C. 53.9
    D. 47
    E. 23.1

▨▨▨▨ SELF-ASSESSMENT ZONE ▨▨▨▨		
CORRECT	**INCORRECT**	**REVIEW THE TAKE**
☐ Lucky Guess	☐ Simple Mistake	
☐ Knew It	☐ Need Practice	

Answer: A

Percentages (Increasing)

A number is increased by 70% and the result is 42.5. What is the number?
- A. 29.75
- B. 27.5
- C. 25
- D. 17
- E. 12.75

Notes:

///// SELF-ASSESSMENT ZONE /////		
CORRECT	**INCORRECT**	**REVIEW THE TIDBIT**
□ Lucky Guess	□ Simple Mistake	
□ Knew It	□ Need Practice	

Do not turn the page until you are ready to proceed with the timed TAKE problem

Percentages (Increasing)

Take 50

A number is increased by 20% and the result is 66. What is the number?

    F. 79.2

    G. 55

    H. 52

    J. 46

    K. 13.2

///// SELF-ASSESSMENT ZONE /////		
CORRECT	**INCORRECT**	**REVIEW THE TAKE**
☐ Lucky Guess	☐ Simple Mistake	
☐ Knew It	☐ Need Practice	

Answer: G

Percentages (Percent Change)

A number is increased by 20% and the resulting number is then decreased by 10%. The final number is what percent of the original number?

    A. 92%

    B. 98%

    C. 100%

    D. 102%

    E. 108%

Notes:

///// SELF-ASSESSMENT ZONE /////		
CORRECT	**INCORRECT**	**REVIEW THE TIDBIT**
☐ Lucky Guess	☐ Simple Mistake	
☐ Knew It	☐ Need Practice	

Do not turn the page until you are ready to proceed with the timed TAKE problem

Percentages (Percent Change)

Take 70

A number is increased by 35% and the resulting number is then decreased by 15%. The final number is what percent of the original number?

    A. 120
    B. 114.75
    C. 110.25
    D. 100
    E. 95.75

▨▨▨ SELF-ASSESSMENT ZONE ▨▨▨		
CORRECT	**INCORRECT**	**REVIEW THE TAKE**
☐ Lucky Guess	☐ Simple Mistake	
☐ Knew It	☐ Need Practice	

Answer: B

Take Quiz 3: Proportions and Percentages

Averages (Finding the Mean)

Matt has earned the following test scores in biology: 84, 92, 75, 76, 90 and 81.
His teacher drops the lowest score before calculating the mean grade. What is
Matt's average grade to the nearest whole number?

   A. 87
   B. 85
   C. 84
   D. 83
   E. 71

Notes:

▨▨▨ SELF-ASSESSMENT ZONE ▨▨▨		
CORRECT	**INCORRECT**	**REVIEW THE TIDBIT**
□ Lucky Guess	□ Simple Mistake	
□ Knew It	□ Need Practice	

Do not turn the page until you are ready to proceed with the timed TAKE problem

Averages (Finding the Mean)

Take 40

To compute a student's grade, Ms. Harwell drops the lowest test score, then finds the mean of the remaining scores. Laura has earned the following test scores: 70, 68, 82, 95 and 75. What is Laura's grade in Ms. Harwell's class to the nearest whole number?

    A. 65
    B. 78
    C. 80
    D. 81
    E. 82

▨▨▨ SELF-ASSESSMENT ZONE ▨▨▨		
CORRECT	**INCORRECT**	**REVIEW THE TAKE**
□ Lucky Guess	□ Simple Mistake	
□ Knew It	□ Need Practice	

Answer: D

Averages (Finding the Mean)

Marlon is bowling in a tournament and has the highest average after 5 games, with scores of 210, 225, 254, 231, and 280. In order to maintain this exact average, what must be Marlon's score for his 6th game?

    F. 200

    G. 210

    H. 231

    J. 240

    K. 245

Notes:

▨▨▨ SELF-ASSESSMENT ZONE ▨▨▨		
CORRECT	**INCORRECT**	**REVIEW THE TIDBIT**
☐ Lucky Guess	☐ Simple Mistake	
☐ Knew It	☐ Need Practice	

Do not turn the page until you are ready to proceed with the timed TAKE problem

Averages (Finding the Mean)

Take 40

So far in Algebra II, Hunter has a 90% average on the first three tests, earning an 82, 91 and 97. What is the lowest score Hunter can earn on the fourth test to maintain this average?

    F. 90
    G. 89
    H. 88
    J. 87
    K. 86

▨▨▨ SELF-ASSESSMENT ZONE ▨▨▨		
CORRECT	**INCORRECT**	**REVIEW THE TAKE**
☐ Lucky Guess	☐ Simple Mistake	
☐ Knew It	☐ Need Practice	

Answer: F

Averages (Finding the Mean)

# of Employees	Salary
3	$38,000
10	$46,000
4	$55,000
1	$92,000

A small marketing firm has the following salary distribution. What is the mean salary to the nearest thousand dollars?

    A. 57,000
    B. 55,000
    C. 53,000
    D. 50,000
    E. 49,000

Notes:

▨▨▨ SELF-ASSESSMENT ZONE ▨▨▨		
CORRECT	**INCORRECT**	**REVIEW THE TIDBIT**
□ Lucky Guess	□ Simple Mistake	
□ Knew It	□ Need Practice	

Do not turn the page until you are ready to proceed with the timed TAKE problem

STOP

Averages (Finding the Mean)

Take 60

The table below shows the total number of goals scored in each of 43 soccer matches in a regional tournament. What is the average number of goals scored per match, to the nearest 0.1 goal?

A. 1.0
B. 2.8
C. 3.0
D. 6.1
E. 17.1

Total number of goals in a match	Number of matches with this total
0	4
1	10
2	5
3	9
4	7
5	5
6	1
7	2

///// SELF-ASSESSMENT ZONE /////		
CORRECT	**INCORRECT**	**REVIEW THE TAKE**
□ Lucky Guess	□ Simple Mistake	
□ Knew It	□ Need Practice	

Answer: B

Median and Mode

- The **median** of an ordered data set is the **middle**.

- The **mode** is the number that occurs **most often**.

Notes:

///// SELF-ASSESSMENT ZONE /////		
CORRECT	**INCORRECT**	**REVIEW THE TIDBIT**
□ Lucky Guess	□ Simple Mistake	
□ Knew It	□ Need Practice	

Do not turn the page until you are ready to proceed with the timed TAKE problem

Median and Mode

Take 30

What is the median of the following data set?

17, 31, 11, 8, 22, 53, 40

    F. 8

    G. 19.5

    H. 22

    J. 26.5

    K. 31

▨▨▨ **SELF-ASSESSMENT ZONE** ▨▨▨		
CORRECT	**INCORRECT**	**REVIEW THE TAKE**
☐ Lucky Guess	☐ Simple Mistake	
☐ Knew It	☐ Need Practice	

Answer: H

Take Quiz 4: Averages

Congratulations!

You completed novice course, class two!

Patience is key. Remember: A jug fills drop by drop.

– Buddha

Novice Course

Class three

- Modeling
- Formulas
- Word Problems

Modeling (Algebraic Translation)

Just like English, Spanish and Mandarin Chinese, **Mathematics** is a language.

*(and the ACT speaks in **Algebra**)*

"**Algebraic Translation**" is the term we will use to translate a phrase written in English to one written in Algebra.

Example: The product of a number, x, squared,
and 7 is 29 becomes:

$$7x^2 = 29$$

Notes:

 SELF-ASSESSMENT ZONE 		
CORRECT	**INCORRECT**	**REVIEW THE TIDBIT**
□ Lucky Guess	□ Simple Mistake	
□ Knew It	□ Need Practice	

Do not turn the page until you are ready to proceed with the timed TAKE problem

Modeling (Algebraic Translation)

Take 35

Which of the following mathematical expressions is equivalent to the verbal expression, "A number, x, squared is 15 more than the product of 2 and x ?"

   A. $2x = 15 + 2x$
   B. $2x = 15 + 2^x$
   C. $x^2 = 15x + 2^x$
   D. $x^2 = 15 + x^2$
   E. $x^2 = 15 + 2x$

///// SELF-ASSESSMENT ZONE /////		
CORRECT	**INCORRECT**	**REVIEW THE TAKE**
☐ Lucky Guess	☐ Simple Mistake	
☐ Knew It	☐ Need Practice	

Answer: E

Modeling (In One Variable)

A window repair company is promoting a deal for spring. They are charging only $24.99 per window after a $30.00 consultation fee. Which of the following is an expression representing the total cost for a customer needing w windows repaired?

F. $24.99w + $30.00

G. $5.01w

H. $54.99w

J. $30.00w + $24.99

K. $749.70w

Notes:

SELF-ASSESSMENT ZONE		
CORRECT	**INCORRECT**	**REVIEW THE TIDBIT**
☐ Lucky Guess	☐ Simple Mistake	
☐ Knew It	☐ Need Practice	

Do not turn the page until you are ready to proceed with the timed TAKE problem

STOP

Modeling (In One Variable)

Take 50

Three high school students decide to start a business making cornhole board games. It will cost them $129.00 to buy a table saw. The wood, paint, fabric, and seeds to make each cornhole set will cost them $20.00. Which of the following expressions could be used to model the total cost of fabricating c cornhole board game sets?

F. $129c + $20

G. $149c

H. $20c + $129

J. $109c

K. $189c

▨▨▨▨ SELF-ASSESSMENT ZONE ▨▨▨▨		
CORRECT	**INCORRECT**	**REVIEW THE TAKE**
□ Lucky Guess	□ Simple Mistake	
□ Knew It	□ Need Practice	

Answer: H

Modeling (In Two Variables)

The Adventure Club is planning an overnight camping trip to Punderson State Park. The nightly fee for camping on the grounds is $5 per person and $8 per vehicle. Which of the following expressions gives the total overnight amount that the Adventure Club will need to pay for p persons and v vehicles?

   F. $5v + 8p$
   G. $5p + 8v$
   H. $5(v + p)$
   J. $13(v + p)$
   K. $5(v + p) + 8p$

Notes:

///// SELF-ASSESSMENT ZONE /////		
CORRECT	**INCORRECT**	**REVIEW THE TIDBIT**
□ Lucky Guess	□ Simple Mistake	
□ Knew It	□ Need Practice	

Do not turn the page until you are ready to proceed with the timed TAKE problem

Modeling (In Two Variables)

Take 50

At the grocery store, it costs a dollars for an apple and m dollars for a mango. The difference in price of 8 apples and 5 mangos is \$3.50. Which of the following equations represents the relationship between a and m?

A. $\frac{8a}{5m} = 3.50$

B. $40am = 3.50$

C. $|8a - 5m| = 3.50$

D. $|8a + 5m| = 3.50$

E. $|5a - 8m| = 3.50$

▨▨▨ SELF-ASSESSMENT ZONE ▨▨▨		
CORRECT	INCORRECT	REVIEW THE TAKE
□ Lucky Guess	□ Simple Mistake	
□ Knew It	□ Need Practice	

Answer: C

Formulas (Plug It In)

For a population that grows at a constant rate of $r\%$ per year, the formula
$P(t) = p_0 \left(1 + \frac{\mu}{100}\right)^t$ models the population t years after an initial population of p_0 people is counted.

The population of Barberton was 26,337 in 2013. Assume the population grows at a constant rate of 3% per year. Which of the following is an expression for the population of Barberton in 2018?

    A. $26{,}337(4)^5$

    B. $26{,}337(1.3)^5$

    C. $26{,}337(1.03)^5$

    D. $(26{,}337 \times 1.3)^5$

    E. $(26{,}337 \times 1.03)^5$

Notes:

SELF-ASSESSMENT ZONE		
CORRECT	**INCORRECT**	**REVIEW THE TIDBIT**
☐ Lucky Guess	☐ Simple Mistake	
☐ Knew It	☐ Need Practice	

Do not turn the page until you are ready to proceed with the timed TAKE problem

Formulas (Plug It In)

Take 50

For a population that decays at a constant rate r per year, the formula $P(t) = p_0(1 - r)^t$ models the population t years after an initial population of p_0 people is counted?

The population of Akron was 199,110 in 2010. Assume the population decays at a constant rate of 2% per year. Which of the following is an expression for the population of Akron in 2017?

   F. $199,110(3)^7$
   G. $199,110(1.2)^7$
   H. $199,110(1.02)^7$
   J. $199,110(.98)^7$
   K. $199,110(.8)^7$

Answer: J

Formulas (Plug It In)

The formula for volume of a cylinder is given by the formula $V = \pi r^2 h$. To the nearest cubic centimeter, what is the volume of the cylinder shown below?

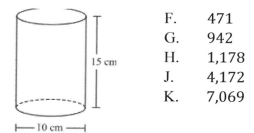

F.   471
G.   942
H.   1,178
J.   4,172
K.   7,069

Notes:

 SELF-ASSESSMENT ZONE		
CORRECT	**INCORRECT**	**REVIEW THE TIDBIT**
☐ Lucky Guess	☐ Simple Mistake	
☐ Knew It	☐ Need Practice	

Do not turn the page until you are ready to proceed with the timed TAKE problem

Formulas (Plug It In)

Take 50

The Enron Company is building a spherical tank to hold shipments of crude oil. The tank will have a radius of 100 feet.

What is the volume of the tank rounded to the nearest cubic foot?

Volume of a sphere: $V = \frac{4}{3}\pi r^3$

    A. 4,188,790

    B. 41,888

    C. 4,189

    D. 419

    E. 41.9

▨ SELF-ASSESSMENT ZONE ▨		
CORRECT	**INCORRECT**	**REVIEW THE TAKE**
☐ Lucky Guess	☐ Simple Mistake	
☐ Knew It	☐ Need Practice	

Answer: A

Take Quiz 5: Modeling and Formulas

Page 176

Word Problems (Combinations)

At a baseball retreat, each camper gets to pick his or her own dinner. There are 2 main entrees, 3 side dishes, and 2 desserts. If a dinner consists of 1 main entrée, 1 side dish, and 1 dessert, how many dinner choices does each camper have?

    A. 3
    B. 6
    C. 7
    D. 12
    E. 24

Notes:

▰▰▰▰ SELF-ASSESSMENT ZONE ▰▰▰▰		
CORRECT	**INCORRECT**	**REVIEW THE TIDBIT**
□ Lucky Guess	□ Simple Mistake	
□ Knew It	□ Need Practice	

Do not turn the page until you are ready to proceed with the timed TAKE problem

Word Problems (Combinations)

Take 40

London brought 2 hats, 4 shirts, 3 pairs of pants, and 2 pairs of shoes to football camp at Ohio State. How many different outfit combinations can he wear in Columbus?

    A. 4
    B. 11
    C. 24
    D. 36
    E. 48

▨▨▨▨ SELF-ASSESSMENT ZONE ▨▨▨▨		
CORRECT	**INCORRECT**	**REVIEW THE TAKE**
☐ Lucky Guess	☐ Simple Mistake	
☐ Knew It	☐ Need Practice	

Answer: E

Word Problems (Combinations)

Laura earns $8.50 per hour regular pay for the first 40 hours she works each week. Laura is paid 1.5 times her regular pay for each hour over 40 hours she works in a week. How much does Laura earn working 44 hours in a week?

 F. $330
 G. $374
 H. $391
 J. $475
 K. $561

Notes:

SELF-ASSESSMENT ZONE		
CORRECT	**INCORRECT**	**REVIEW THE TIDBIT**
☐ Lucky Guess	☐ Simple Mistake	
☐ Knew It	☐ Need Practice	

Do not turn the page until you are ready to proceed with the timed TAKE problem

Word Problems (Combinations)

Take 60

You and your two best friends are planning a road trip to Florida. A Mustang convertible costs $125 a day to rent plus 11.5 cents per mile. How much will your 7-day road trip cost, if you drive 2,900 miles total?

    F. $34,239.00

    G. $3,043.50

    H. $1,208.50

    J. $875.00

    K. $205.50

▨▨▨▨ SELF-ASSESSMENT ZONE ▨▨▨▨		
CORRECT	**INCORRECT**	**REVIEW THE TAKE**
□ Lucky Guess	□ Simple Mistake	
□ Knew It	□ Need Practice	

Answer: H

Word Problems (Combining Fractions)

Dana is training for a half-marathon and is running 4 times per week. On Monday, she ran $4\frac{2}{3}$ miles, and on Tuesday, she ran $7\frac{3}{4}$ miles. On Thursday and Saturday, she ran $10\frac{2}{3}$ and 2 miles, respectively. What was her total mileage for the week?

F. $23\frac{1}{12}$

G. $23\frac{7}{10}$

H. $25\frac{1}{12}$

J. $25\frac{1}{3}$

K. $25\frac{5}{12}$

Notes:

▨▨▨▨ SELF-ASSESSMENT ZONE ▨▨▨▨		
CORRECT	**INCORRECT**	**REVIEW THE TIDBIT**
□ Lucky Guess	□ Simple Mistake	
□ Knew It	□ Need Practice	

Do not turn the page until you are ready to proceed with the timed TAKE problem

STOP

Word Problems (Combining Fractions)

Take 70

Blake worked $5\frac{1}{2}$ hours on Monday, $3\frac{3}{4}$ on Tuesday, $4\frac{1}{4}$ hours on Wednesday, 3 hours on Thursday and $4\frac{1}{2}$ hours on Friday. How many hours did Blake work for the week?

A. 21
B. $12\frac{1}{4}$
C. $12\frac{1}{2}$
D. $12\frac{3}{4}$
E. 13

⬛▨⬛ SELF-ASSESSMENT ZONE ⬛▨⬛		
CORRECT	**INCORRECT**	**REVIEW THE TAKE**
□ Lucky Guess	□ Simple Mistake	
□ Knew It	□ Need Practice	

Answer: A

Take Quiz 6: Word Problems
Page 180

Congratulations!

You completed the novice course!

Success doesn't come without education and hard work.

— Sandy Martinez

Intermediate course

Class one

- Linear Functions
- Quadratic Functions

Linear Functions (Graphs)

Which graph represents the function $f(x) = -2x + 1$?

A.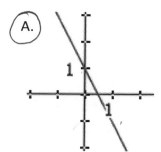

B.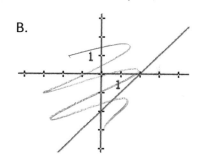

C.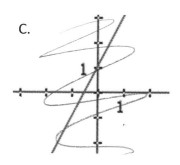

D.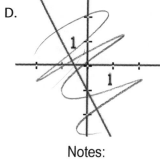

E.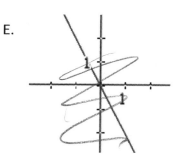

Notes:

 SELF-ASSESSMENT ZONE		
CORRECT	**INCORRECT**	**REVIEW THE TIDBIT**
☐ Lucky Guess	☐ Simple Mistake	
☑ Knew It	☐ Need Practice	

Do not turn the page until you are ready to proceed with the timed TAKE problem

STOP

Linear Functions (Graphs)

Take 30
Which graph represents the function $y = x - 3$?

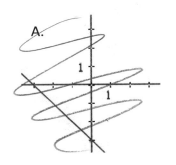 A.

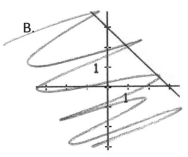 B.

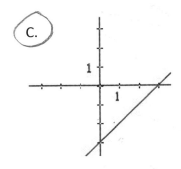 C.

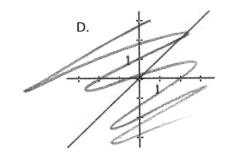 D.

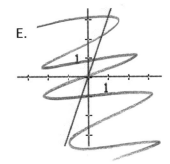 E.

▨▨▨ SELF-ASSESSMENT ZONE ▨▨▨		
CORRECT	**INCORRECT**	**REVIEW THE TAKE**
☐ Lucky Guess	☐ Simple Mistake	
☑ Knew It	☐ Need Practice	

Answer: C

Linear Functions (Graphs)

Which graph represents the function $f(x) = 2x + y = 3$?

$y = 2x + y = 3$

$-2x$

$y = -2x + 3$

F.

G.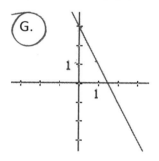

H.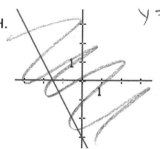

J.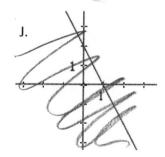

K.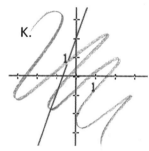

+

Notes:

///// SELF-ASSESSMENT ZONE /////		
CORRECT	**INCORRECT**	**REVIEW THE TIDBIT**
☐ Lucky Guess	☐ Simple Mistake	
☑ Knew It	☐ Need Practice	

Do not turn the page until you are ready to proceed with the timed TAKE problem

Linear Functions (Graphs)

Take 40

Which graph represents the function $2x - 3y = 6$?

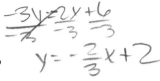

$-3y = 2x + 6$
$\dfrac{}{-3} \quad \dfrac{-3}{} \quad \dfrac{6}{3}$
$y = -\dfrac{2}{3}x + 2$

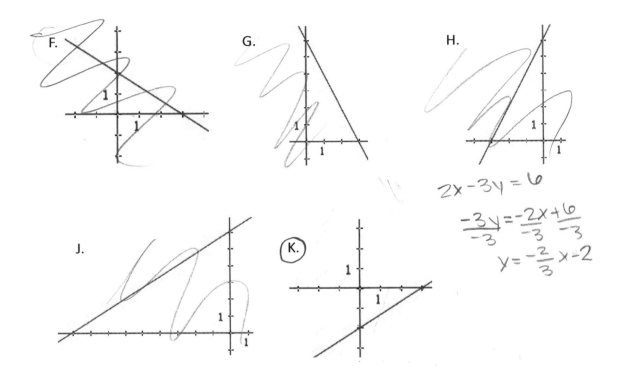

$2x - 3y = 6$

$\dfrac{-3y}{-3} = \dfrac{-2x}{-3} + \dfrac{6}{-3}$

$y = -\dfrac{2}{3}x - 2$

▨▨▨▨	**SELF-ASSESSMENT ZONE**	▨▨▨▨
CORRECT	**INCORRECT**	**REVIEW THE TAKE**
□ Lucky Guess	☑ Simple Mistake	
☑ Knew It	□ Need Practice	

Answer: K

Linear Functions (Slope)

What is the slope of the line that passes through $(5,1)$ and $(2,7)$?

$x_1\ y_1 \qquad x_2\ y_2$

(A.) -2

B. $-\frac{4}{5}$

C. $-\frac{1}{2}$

D. $\frac{1}{2}$

E. 2

$$\frac{7-1}{2-5}$$

$$\frac{6}{-3}$$

Notes:

▨▨▨▨ SELF-ASSESSMENT ZONE ▨▨▨▨		
CORRECT	**INCORRECT**	**REVIEW THE TIDBIT**
☐ Lucky Guess	☐ Simple Mistake	
☑ Knew It	☐ Need Practice	

Do not turn the page until you are ready to proceed with the timed TAKE problem

STOP

Linear Functions (Slope)

Take 40
What is the slope of the line that passes through (-3,0) and (-7,2)?

- A. 5
- B. $\frac{1}{2}$
- C. $\frac{1}{5}$
- D. $-\frac{1}{2}$
- E. -2

$$\frac{2-0}{-7+3}$$

$$\frac{2}{-4}$$

▨▨▨ SELF-ASSESSMENT ZONE ▨▨▨		
CORRECT	**INCORRECT**	**REVIEW THE TAKE**
☐ Lucky Guess	☐ Simple Mistake	
☑ Knew It	☐ Need Practice	

Linear Functions (Slope)

What is the equation of the line parallel to $4x - 2y = 3$ that passes through (1,-5)?

   F. $y = 4x - 9$
   G. $y = 4x + 1$
   (H.) $y = 2x - 7$
   J. $y = 2x - 1.5$
   K. $y = 2x + 3$

$$-2y = -4x + 3$$
$$\frac{-2y}{-2} = \frac{-4x}{-2} + \frac{3}{-2}$$
$$y = 2x - \frac{3}{2}$$

Notes:

$$y = mx + b$$
$$-5 = 2(1) + b$$
$$-5 = 2 + b$$
$$\quad\ -2$$
$$-7 = b$$

$$y - y_1 = x(x$$

$$y - y_1 = m(x - x_1)$$
$$y - 5 = 2(x + 1)$$
$$y - 5 = 2x + 2$$
$$+5$$
$$y = 2x + 7$$

▨▨▨ SELF-ASSESSMENT ZONE ▨▨▨		
CORRECT	**INCORRECT**	**REVIEW THE TIDBIT**
☐ Lucky Guess	☐ Simple Mistake	
☑ Knew It	☐ Need Practice	

Do not turn the page until you are ready to proceed with the timed TAKE problem

Linear Functions (Slope)

Take 40

What is the equation of the line parallel to $6x + 3y = 4$ that passes through (-1,2)?

F. $y = -6x + 2$
G. $y = -2x$
H. $y = -2x - 7$
J. $y = 6x$
K. $y = 6x + 2$

$$\frac{3y}{3} = \frac{-6x}{3} + \frac{4}{3}$$

$$y = -2x + \frac{4}{3}$$

$$2 = -2(-1) + b$$
$$2 = 2 + b$$
$$\underline{-2}$$
$$0 = b$$

▨▨▨▨ SELF-ASSESSMENT ZONE ▨▨▨▨		
CORRECT	**INCORRECT**	**REVIEW THE TAKE**
☐ Lucky Guess	☐ Simple Mistake	
☑ Knew It	☐ Need Practice	

Answer: G

70

Linear Functions (Slope)

What is the equation of the line perpendicular to $x - 2y = 4$ that passes through (4,0)?

~~A. $y = x + 4$~~
~~B. $y = x - 4$~~
C. $y = 2x + 8$
(D.) $y = 2x - 8$
~~E. $y = -2x + 8$~~

$$\frac{-2y}{-2} = \frac{-x}{-2} + \frac{4}{-2}$$

$$y = -0.5x - 2$$

$$0 = -0.5(4) + b$$
$$0 = -2 + b$$
$$ +2$$
$$2 = b$$

$$0 = 2(4) + b$$
$$0 = 8 + b$$
$$ -8$$
$$-8 = b$$

Notes:

![SELF-ASSESSMENT ZONE] SELF-ASSESSMENT ZONE		
CORRECT	**INCORRECT**	**REVIEW THE TIDBIT**
☐ Lucky Guess	☐ Simple Mistake	
☑ Knew It	☐ Need Practice	

Do not turn the page until you are ready to proceed with the timed TAKE problem

STOP

71

Linear Functions (Slope)

Take 40

What is the equation of the line perpendicular to $x + 3y = 12$ that passes through $(0,-3)$?

A. ~~$y = x - 3$~~
B. ~~$y = -x - 3$~~
C. $y = 3x - 3$
D. $y = 3x$
E. ~~$y = -\frac{1}{3}x + 8$~~

$$\frac{3y = -x + 12}{3} \quad \frac{3}{3}$$

$$y = \frac{-x}{3} + 4$$

$$\frac{3}{1}x$$

$$\boxed{3x}$$

$$-3 = 3(0) + b$$

$$-3 = b$$

⬛⬛⬛⬛ SELF-ASSESSMENT ZONE ⬛⬛⬛⬛		
CORRECT	**INCORRECT**	**REVIEW THE TAKE**
☐ Lucky Guess	☐ Simple Mistake	
☑ Knew It	☐ Need Practice	

Answer: C

Linear Functions (Slope)

What is the value of k in the equation $y = -\frac{4}{3}kx - 2$ if its graph is parallel to the line whose equation is $2x - 3y = -3$?

F. -2

G. $-\frac{3}{2}$

H. $-\frac{1}{2}$

J. $\frac{1}{2}$

K. $\frac{3}{2}$

$$-\frac{3y}{-3} = \frac{-2x - 3}{-3 \ -3}$$

$$y = \frac{2}{3}x + 1$$

$$-\frac{2}{3} \div -\frac{4}{3} = \frac{1}{2}$$

Notes:

![] SELF-ASSESSMENT ZONE ![]		
CORRECT	**INCORRECT**	**REVIEW THE TIDBIT**
☐ Lucky Guess	☐ Simple Mistake	
☑ Knew It	☐ Need Practice	

Do not turn the page until you are ready to proceed with the timed TAKE problem

STOP

Linear Functions (Slope)

Take 40

What is the value of k in the equation $y = -\frac{1}{3}kx + 3$ if its graph is perpendicular to the line whose equation is $x + 3y = 9$?

- F. -9
- G. -3
- H. -1
- J. 1
- K. 3

$$\frac{3y}{3} = \frac{-x}{3} + \frac{9}{3}$$

$$y = -\frac{1}{3}x + 3$$

$$y = 3x + 3$$

$$-\frac{1}{3}x \quad -\frac{1}{3} = \frac{1}{9}$$

-9

perp opposite sign reciprocal

▨▨▨ SELF-ASSESSMENT ZONE ▨▨▨		
CORRECT	INCORRECT	REVIEW THE TAKE
☐ Lucky Guess	☐ Simple Mistake	
☑ Knew It	☐ Need Practice	

Answer: F

Quadratic Functions (Graphing)

The parabola most closely resembles the graph of which of the following equations?

A. $y = x^2 + 1$
B. $y = x^2 - 1$
C. $y = 2x^2$
D. $y = -x^2 - 1$
E. $y = x^3 - 1$

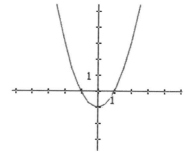

Notes:

		
CORRECT	**INCORRECT**	**REVIEW THE TIDBIT**
☐ Lucky Guess	☐ Simple Mistake	
☑ Knew It	☐ Need Practice	

Do not turn the page until you are ready to proceed with the timed TAKE problem

STOP

Quadratic Functions (Graphing)

Take 40

The parabola most closely resembles the graph of which of the following equations?

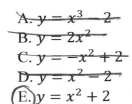

A. $y = x^3 - 2$
B. $y = 2x^2$
C. $y = -x^2 + 2$
D. $y = x^2 - 2$
E. $y = x^2 + 2$

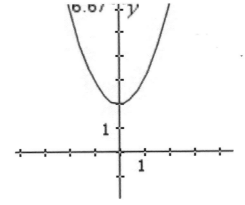

▨▨▨ SELF-ASSESSMENT ZONE ▨▨▨		
CORRECT	**INCORRECT**	**REVIEW THE TAKE**
☐ Lucky Guess	☐ Simple Mistake	
☑ Knew It	☐ Need Practice	

Answer: E

Quadratic Functions (Factoring)

What values of x are the solutions to the equation $x^2 + 3x = 18$?

~~A. −3 and 6~~
B. −6 and 3
~~C. 0 and −3~~
D. 0 and −6
E. 6 and 3

Notes:

 SELF-ASSESSMENT ZONE		
CORRECT	**INCORRECT**	**REVIEW THE TIDBIT**
□ Lucky Guess	□ Simple Mistake	
□ Knew It	☑ Need Practice	

Do not turn the page until you are ready to proceed with the timed TAKE problem

77

Quadratic Functions (Factoring)

Take 40

What values of x are the solutions to the equation $x^2 - 9x = -14$?

F. 7 and 2
G. -7 and -2
H. 0 and -7
J. 0 and 2
K. -9 and -14

$0^2 - 9(-7) =$

 SELF-ASSESSMENT ZONE 		
CORRECT	**INCORRECT**	**REVIEW THE TAKE**
☐ Lucky Guess	☐ Simple Mistake	
☐ Knew It	☐ Need Practice	

Answer: F

Take Quiz 7: Linear and Quadratic Functions

Page 184

Congratulations!

You completed intermediate course, class one!

If we aren't supposed to make mistakes, why did someone invent erasers?

— Matt Deevers

$$2x^2 + 5x - 12$$

$$\left(x + \frac{8}{2}\right)\left(x - \frac{3}{2}\right)$$

$$(x+4)\left(x - \tfrac{3}{2}\right)$$

$$(x+4)(2x-3)$$

-24

a·c

8   -3

6

5

Intermediate Course

Class two

- The Quadrants
- Midpoints and Distance
- Rectangles
- Circles
- Triangles

The Quadrants (A Point)

If point M has a nonzero x-coordinate and a nonzero, y-coordinate, and the y-coordinate is negative, then point M must be located in which of the 4 quadrants labeled below?

A. I only
B. III only
C. IV only
D. II or III only
E. III or IV only

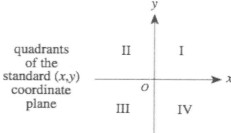

quadrants
of the
standard (x,y)
coordinate
plane

Notes:

 SELF-ASSESSMENT ZONE ///////		
CORRECT	**INCORRECT**	**REVIEW THE TIDBIT**
□ Lucky Guess	□ Simple Mistake	
□ Knew It	□ Need Practice	

Do not turn the page until you are ready to proceed with the timed TAKE problem

The Quadrants (A Point)

Take 25

If point T has a nonzero x-coordinate and a nonzero y-coordinate, and the coordinates have opposite signs, then point T must be located in which of the 4 quadrants labeled below?

A. I only
B. III only
C. I or III only
D. I or IV only
E. II or IV only

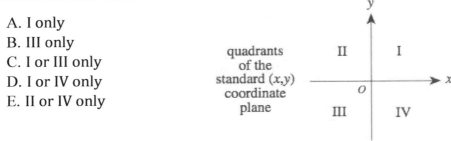

quadrants of the standard (x,y) coordinate plane

SELF-ASSESSMENT ZONE		
CORRECT	**INCORRECT**	**REVIEW THE TAKE**
☐ Lucky Guess	☐ Simple Mistake	
☐ Knew It	☐ Need Practice	

Answer: E

The Quadrants (A Line)

The line $3x + 2y = 6$ passes through which of the 4 quadrants, as labeled below?

A. I and II only
B. I and IV only
C. II and IV only
D. I , II, or IV only
E. II, III, or IV only

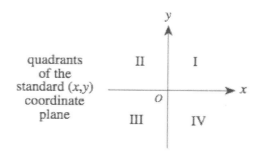

Notes:

<div style="text-align:center">/// SELF-ASSESSMENT ZONE ///</div>		
CORRECT	**INCORRECT**	**REVIEW THE TIDBIT**
□ Lucky Guess	□ Simple Mistake	
□ Knew It	□ Need Practice	

Do not turn the page until you are ready to proceed with the timed TAKE problem

The Quadrants (A Line)

Take 50

The line $4x - 2y = 8$ passes through which of the 4 quadrants, as labeled below?

F. I and II only
G. I and IV only
H. II and IV only
J. I, II, and III only
K. I, III, and IV only

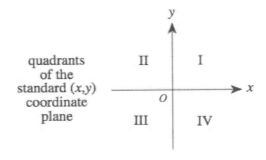

quadrants
of the
standard (x,y)
coordinate
plane

		
CORRECT	**INCORRECT**	**REVIEW THE TAKE**
□ Lucky Guess	□ Simple Mistake	
□ Knew It	□ Need Practice	

Answer: K

Midpoint and Distance (Finding the Midpoint)

In the standard *(x,y)* coordinate plane, the endpoints of a segment are at (-4,4) and (7,2). What are the coordinates of the midpoint of the segment?

   F. (3,6)

   G. (1.5,3)

   H. (−5.5,1)

   J. (1.5,6)

   K. (3,3)

Notes:

/////// SELF-ASSESSMENT ZONE ///////		
CORRECT	**INCORRECT**	**REVIEW THE TIDBIT**
□ Lucky Guess	□ Simple Mistake	
□ Knew It	□ Need Practice	

Do not turn the page until you are ready to proceed with the timed TAKE problem

Midpoint and Distance (Finding the Midpoint)

Take 30

In the standard *(x,y)* coordinate plane, the endpoints of a segment are at (1,8) and (5,2). What are the coordinates of the midpoint of the segment)?

   A. (3,5)
   B. (−4,6)
   C. (−2,3)
   D. (6,10)
   E. (3,10)

▨▨▨ SELF-ASSESSMENT ZONE ▨▨▨		
CORRECT	**INCORRECT**	**REVIEW THE TAKE**
□ Lucky Guess	□ Simple Mistake	
□ Knew It	□ Need Practice	

Answer: A

Midpoint and Distance (Finding the Endpoint)

In the standard *(x,y)* coordinate plane, the coordinates of one endpoint of a segment are (-3,2). The midpoint of the segment is (1,3). What are the coordinates of the other endpoint of the segment?

    A. (4,1)
    B. (5,6)
    C. (−1,2.5)
    D. (5,4)
    E. (5,1)

Notes:

▨▨▨ SELF-ASSESSMENT ZONE ▨▨▨		
CORRECT	**INCORRECT**	**REVIEW THE TIDBIT**
☐ Lucky Guess	☐ Simple Mistake	
☐ Knew It	☐ Need Practice	

Do not turn the page until you are ready to proceed with the timed TAKE problem

STOP

Midpoint and Distance (Finding the Endpoint)

Take 45

In the standard *(x,y)* coordinate plane, the coordinates of one endpoint of a segment are (4,7). The midpoint of the segment is (3,-2). What are the coordinates of the other endpoint of the segment?

F. $(-1,-9)$

G. $(3.5,2.5)$

H. $(3.5,-11)$

J. $(2,-11)$

K. $(2,-9)$

▨▨ SELF-ASSESSMENT ZONE ▨▨		
CORRECT	INCORRECT	REVIEW THE TAKE
□ Lucky Guess	□ Simple Mistake	
□ Knew It	□ Need Practice	

Answer: J

Midpoint and Distance (Distance Formula)

If point P has coordinates (-2,2) and point Q has coordinates (2,0), what is the distance from point P to point Q?

A. -4

B. $2\sqrt{5}$

C. $4\sqrt{5}$

D. 4

E. 6

Notes:

Midpoint and Distance (Distance Formula)

Take 60

If point P has coordinates (3,-2) and point Q has coordinates (-1,2), what is PQ?

A. 4
B. $2\sqrt{5}$
C. $4\sqrt{2}$
D. 8
E. $4\sqrt{6}$

▨▨▨ SELF-ASSESSMENT ZONE ▨▨▨		
CORRECT	INCORRECT	REVIEW THE TAKE
□ Lucky Guess	□ Simple Mistake	
□ Knew It	□ Need Practice	

Answer: C

Rectangles (Vertex of a Square)

The sides of a square are 5cm long. One vertex of the square is at (5,0). On a square coordinate grid marked in centimeter units, which of the following points could also be the vertex of the square?

A. $(-5,-5)$
B. $(-5,0)$
C. $(0,5)$
D. $(2.5,0)$
E. $(0,-7)$

Notes:

		
CORRECT	**INCORRECT**	**REVIEW THE TIDBIT**
☐ Lucky Guess	☐ Simple Mistake	
☐ Knew It	☐ Need Practice	

Do not turn the page until you are ready to proceed with the timed TAKE problem

STOP

Rectangles (Vertex of a Square)

Take 40

The sides of a square are 2ft long. One vertex of the square is at (2,2). On a square coordinate grid marked in feet units, which of the following points could also be the vertex of the square?

F. $(-2,2)$
G. $(2,0)$
H. $(-2,0)$
J. $(4,-2)$
K. $(4,1)$

▨▨▨ SELF-ASSESSMENT ZONE ▨▨▨		
CORRECT	**INCORRECT**	**REVIEW THE TAKE**
□ Lucky Guess	□ Simple Mistake	
□ Knew It	□ Need Practice	

Answer: G

Rectangles (Vertex of a Rectangle)

In the standard *(x,y)* coordinate plane shown below, three vertices of a rectangle are shown. Which of the following is a possible coordinate of the fourth vertex?

A. $(3, -2)$
B. $(0, -4)$
C. $(-1, -3)$
D. $(-3, 2)$
E. $(-2, 3)$

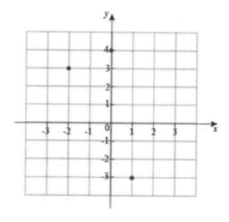

Notes:

Do not turn the page until you are ready to proceed with the timed TAKE problem

STOP

Rectangles (Vertex of a Rectangle)

Take 50

In the standard *(x,y)* coordinate plane shown below, three vertices of a rectangle are shown. Which of the following is a possible coordinate of the fourth vertex?

F. (5,0)
G. (5,−1)
H. (−1,5)
J. (0,6)
K. (6,0)

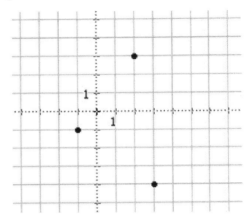

▨▨▨ SELF-ASSESSMENT ZONE ▨▨▨		
CORRECT	**INCORRECT**	**REVIEW THE TAKE**
☐ Lucky Guess	☐ Simple Mistake	
☐ Knew It	☐ Need Practice	

Take Quiz 8: All about Coordinates

Page 188

94

Circles (Graph and Equation)

The circle graphed below has center (4,-3) and is tangent to the *x-axis* at (4,0). What is the equation of the circle?

A. $(x - 3)^2 + (y + 4)^2 = 3$
B. $(x - 3)^2 + (y + 4)^2 = 9$
C. $(x - 4)^2 + (y + 3)^2 = 3$
D. $(x - 4)^2 + (y + 3)^2 = 9$
E. $(x + 3)^2 + (y - 4)^2 = 9$

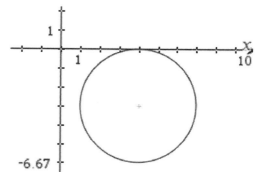

Notes:

Do not turn the page until you are ready to proceed with the timed TAKE problem

Circles (Graph and Equation)

Take 50

The circle graphed below has center (0,4) and is tangent to the *x-axis* at (0,0).
What is the equation of the circle?

F. $x^2 + (y - 4)^2 = 16$
G. $x^2 + (y - 4)^2 = 4$
H. $(x - 4)^2 + y^2 = 16$
J. $(x - 4)^2 + y^2 = 4$
K. $x^2 + (y + 4)^2 = 16$

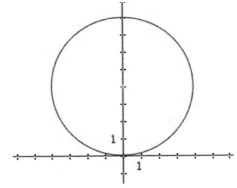

▨▨▨▨ SELF-ASSESSMENT ZONE ▨▨▨▨		
CORRECT	**INCORRECT**	**REVIEW THE TAKE**
□ Lucky Guess	□ Simple Mistake	
□ Knew It	□ Need Practice	

Tidbit 2.2.9   1 Minute

Circles (Exploring the Equation)

In the standard (x, y) coordinate plane, a circle has the equation $(x - 3)^2 + y^2 = 26$. What is the radius and center for the circle?

Radius	Center
A. $\sqrt{26}$	$(-3, 0)$
B. $\sqrt{26}$	$(3, 0)$
C. 13	$(-3, 0)$
D. 26	$(-3, 0)$
E. 26	$(3, 0)$

Notes:

SELF-ASSESSMENT ZONE		
CORRECT	**INCORRECT**	**REVIEW THE TIDBIT**
☐ Lucky Guess	☐ Simple Mistake	
☐ Knew It	☐ Need Practice	

Do not turn the page until you are ready to proceed with the timed TAKE problem

97

Circles (Exploring the Equation)

Take 50

In the standard (x, y) coordinate plane, a circle has the equation $(x + 2)^2 + (y - 5)^2 = 49$. What is the radius and center of the circle?

	Radius	Center
A.	7	$(2, -5)$
B.	7	$(-2, 5)$
C.	14	$(2, -5)$
D.	49	$(2, -5)$
E.	49	$(-2, 5)$

///// SELF-ASSESSMENT ZONE /////		
CORRECT	**INCORRECT**	**REVIEW THE TAKE**
☐ Lucky Guess	☐ Simple Mistake	
☐ Knew It	☐ Need Practice	

Answer: B

Triangles (Area)

The triangle below is graphed in the standard (x,y) coordinate plane. What is the area, in square units?

A. 16
B. 9
C. 8
D. 6
E. 4.5

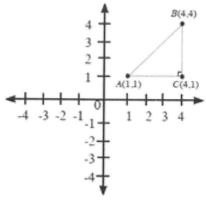

Notes:

<table>
<tr><td colspan="3" align="center">▨▨▨ SELF-ASSESSMENT ZONE ▨▨▨</td></tr>
<tr><td align="center">CORRECT</td><td align="center">INCORRECT</td><td align="center">REVIEW THE TIDBIT</td></tr>
<tr><td>☐ Lucky Guess</td><td>☐ Simple Mistake</td><td rowspan="2"></td></tr>
<tr><td>☐ Knew It</td><td>☐ Need Practice</td></tr>
</table>

Do not turn the page until you are ready to proceed with the timed TAKE problem

Triangles (Area)

Take 50

The triangle below is graphed in the standard (x,y) coordinate plane. What is the area, in square units?

F. 24
G. 15
H. 12
J. 7.5
K. 6

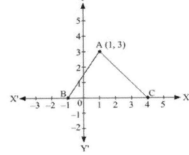

▨▨▨▨ SELF-ASSESSMENT ZONE ▨▨▨▨		
CORRECT	**INCORRECT**	**REVIEW THE TAKE**
□ Lucky Guess	□ Simple Mistake	
□ Knew It	□ Need Practice	

Answer: J

Take Quiz 9: Circles and Triangles in the Coordinate Plane

Page 192

Congratulations!

You completed intermediate course, class two!

You fail, and then what? Life goes on. It's only when you risk failure that you discover things.

— Lupita Nyong'o

Intermediate course

Class three

- Logarithms
- Exponential Equations
- Head Scratchers
- Substitution

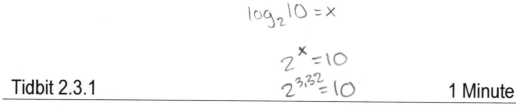

$$\log_2 10 = x$$
$$2^x = 10$$
$$2^{3.32} = 10$$

Tidbit 2.3.1   1 Minute

Logarithms

What is $\log_3 81$?

A. 2
B. 3
C. 4
D. 27
E. 81

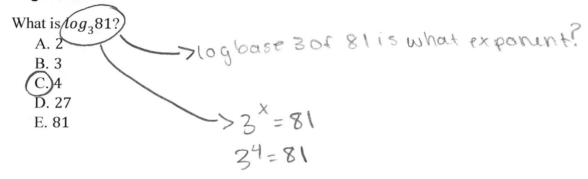

→ log base 3 of 81 is what exponent?

→ $3^x = 81$
$3^4 = 81$

Notes:

$$\log_{base} ans = exponent$$

convert to exponent form
base^{exp} = ans.

⚠️ SELF-ASSESSMENT ZONE ⚠️		
CORRECT	**INCORRECT**	**REVIEW THE TIDBIT**
☐ Lucky Guess	☐ Simple Mistake	
☑ Knew It	☐ Need Practice	

Do not turn the page until you are ready to proceed with the timed TAKE problem

Logarithms

Take 45

What is $\log_4 16$?

(F.) 2

G. 3

H. 10

J. 12

K. 16

▨▨▨ SELF-ASSESSMENT ZONE ▨▨▨		
CORRECT	**INCORRECT**	**REVIEW THE TAKE**
□ Lucky Guess	□ Simple Mistake	
□ Knew It	□ Need Practice	

Answer: F

Exponential Equations

In the real numbers, what is the solution of the equation $4^{2x+1} = 32^{x-3}$?

 F. -2
 G. 2
 H. 4
 J. $\dfrac{25}{6}$
 K. 17

Notes:

 SELF-ASSESSMENT ZONE 		
CORRECT	**INCORRECT**	**REVIEW THE TIDBIT**
□ Lucky Guess	□ Simple Mistake	
□ Knew It	□ Need Practice	

Do not turn the page until you are ready to proceed with the timed TAKE problem

Exponential Equations

Take 70

In the real numbers, what is the solution of the equation $8^{1-x} = 4^{3x+2}$?

    A. -9

    B. -4

    C. $-\dfrac{3}{7}$

    D. $-\dfrac{1}{4}$

    E. $-\dfrac{1}{9}$

▨▨▨▨ SELF-ASSESSMENT ZONE ▨▨▨▨		
CORRECT	**INCORRECT**	**REVIEW THE TAKE**
☐ Lucky Guess	☐ Simple Mistake	
☐ Knew It	☐ Need Practice	

Answer: E

Head Scratchers

If $a < b$, then $|a - b|$ is equivalent to which of the following?

    F. $a + b$
    G. $-(a + b)$
    H. $\sqrt{a - b}$
    J. $a - b$
    K. $-(a - b)$

Notes:

▨▨▨ SELF-ASSESSMENT ZONE ▨▨▨		
CORRECT	**INCORRECT**	**REVIEW THE TIDBIT**
☐ Lucky Guess	☐ Simple Mistake	
☐ Knew It	☐ Need Practice	

Do not turn the page until you are ready to proceed with the timed TAKE problem

Head Scratchers

Take 60

If $a > b$, then $|a - b|$ is equivalent to which of the following?

F. $a + b$
G. $-(a + b)$
H. $\sqrt{a - b}$
J. $a - b$
K. $-(a - b)$

▨▨▨ SELF-ASSESSMENT ZONE ▨▨▨		
CORRECT	**INCORRECT**	**REVIEW THE TAKE**
□ Lucky Guess	□ Simple Mistake	
□ Knew It	□ Need Practice	

Answer: J

Head Scratchers

If x and y are real numbers such that $x > 1$ and $y < -1$ then which of the following inequalities *must* be true?

A. $\frac{x}{y} > 1$

B. $|x|^2 > |y|$

C. $\frac{x}{3} - 5 > \frac{y}{3} - 5$

D. $x^2 + 1 > y^2 + 1$

E. $x^{-2} > y^{-2}$

Notes:

CORRECT	**INCORRECT**	**REVIEW THE TIDBIT**
☐ Lucky Guess	☐ Simple Mistake	
☐ Knew It	☐ Need Practice	

Do not turn the page until you are ready to proceed with the timed TAKE problem

STOP

Head Scratchers

Take 70

If x and y are real numbers such that $x > 0$ and $y \leq 0$ then which of the following inequalities *must* be true?

F. $\frac{x}{y} < 0$

G. $\frac{y}{x} < 0$

H. $\frac{x}{y} \geq 0$

J. $\frac{y}{x} \leq 0$

K. $\frac{x}{y} \leq 0$

SELF-ASSESSMENT ZONE		
CORRECT	**INCORRECT**	**REVIEW THE TAKE**
□ Lucky Guess	□ Simple Mistake	
□ Knew It	□ Need Practice	

Answer: H

Take Quiz 10: Advanced Algebra Topics
Page 196

STOP

Substitution (Integration Substitution)

What is the value of the expression $(a - b)^2$ when $a = 2$ and $b = -5$?

    A. 3
    B. 6
    C. 9
    D. 14
    E. 49

Notes:

<div style="text-align:center">▨▨▨ SELF-ASSESSMENT ZONE ▨▨▨</div>		
CORRECT	**INCORRECT**	**REVIEW THE TIDBIT**
☐ Lucky Guess	☐ Simple Mistake	
☐ Knew It	☐ Need Practice	

Do not turn the page until you are ready to proceed with the timed TAKE problem

STOP

Substitution (Integration Substitution)

Take 30

What is the value of the expression $2(x - y)^2$ when $x = 1$ and $y = -3$?

    A. 8
    B. 16
    C. 25
    D. 32
    E. 64

▨▨▨ SELF-ASSESSMENT ZONE ▨▨▨		
CORRECT	**INCORRECT**	**REVIEW THE TAKE**
☐ Lucky Guess	☐ Simple Mistake	
☐ Knew It	☐ Need Practice	

Answer: D

Substitution (Evaluating a Function)

$f(x)$ is defined as $f(x) = 3x^2 + 1$. What is $f(-2)$?

    F. -11
    G. 7
    H. 13
    J. 19
    K. 37

Notes:

▨▨▨ **SELF-ASSESSMENT ZONE** ▨▨▨		
CORRECT	**INCORRECT**	**REVIEW THE TIDBIT**
☐ Lucky Guess	☐ Simple Mistake	
☐ Knew It	☐ Need Practice	

Do not turn the page until you are ready to proceed with the timed TAKE problem

STOP

Substitution (Evaluating a Function)

Take 30

$g(x)$ is defined as $g(x) = -2x^2$. What is g(3)?

    F. -18
    G. -12
    H. 12
    J. 18
    K. 36

▨▨▨▨ SELF-ASSESSMENT ZONE ▨▨▨▨		
CORRECT	**INCORRECT**	**REVIEW THE TAKE**
□ Lucky Guess	□ Simple Mistake	
□ Knew It	□ Need Practice	

Answer: F

Substitution (Function Composition)

Given $f(x) = 2x - 11$ and $g(x) = x^2 + 5$, what is the expression for $f(g(x))$?

    A. $4x^2 - 44x + 126$
    B. $2x^2 - 1$
    C. $2x^2 - 6$
    D. $x^2 + 2x - 6$
    E. $-x^2 + 2x + 6$

Notes:

///// SELF-ASSESSMENT ZONE /////		
CORRECT	**INCORRECT**	**REVIEW THE TIDBIT**
☐ Lucky Guess	☐ Simple Mistake	
☐ Knew It	☐ Need Practice	

Do not turn the page until you are ready to proceed with the timed TAKE problem

Substitution (Function Composition)

Take 50

Given $f(x) = 3x - 1$ and $g(x) = x^2 + 1$, what is the expression for $f(g(x))$?

  A. $x^2 + 3x$
  B. $3x^2$
  C. $3x^2 + 2$
  D. $9x^2 + 2$
  E. $9x^2 - 6x + 2$

▨▨▨ SELF-ASSESSMENT ZONE ▨▨▨		
CORRECT	**INCORRECT**	**REVIEW THE TAKE**
☐ Lucky Guess	☐ Simple Mistake	
☐ Knew It	☐ Need Practice	

Answer: C

Take Quiz 11: Substitution

Page 200

Congratulations!

You completed the intermediate course!

The beautiful thing about learning is that no one can take it away from you.

— B.B. King

Advanced course

Class one

- Triangles
- Polygons
- Circles

Triangles (Pythagorean Theorem)

In the isosceles right triangle ABC, what is the length of $\overline{AC}$?

A. 200
B. $10\sqrt{2}$
C. $50\sqrt{2}$
D. 100
E. $2\sqrt{10}$

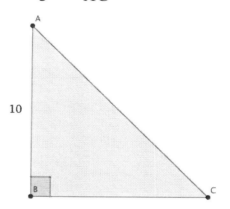

Notes:

 SELF-ASSESSMENT ZONE 		
CORRECT	**INCORRECT**	**REVIEW THE TIDBIT**
□ Lucky Guess	□ Simple Mistake	
□ Knew It	□ Need Practice	

Do not turn the page until you are ready to proceed with the timed TAKE problem

STOP

Triangles (Pythagorean Theorem)

Take 50

In a triangle ABC, AC = 20 and AB = 16. What is the length of side BC?

F. 144
G. $4\sqrt{41}$
H. 16
J. 12
K. $10\sqrt{3}$

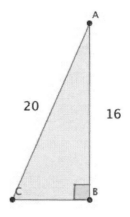

▨▨▨▨ SELF-ASSESSMENT ZONE ▨▨▨▨		
CORRECT	**INCORRECT**	**REVIEW THE TAKE**
□ Lucky Guess	□ Simple Mistake	
□ Knew It	□ Need Practice	

Answer: J

Triangles (Area of)

What is the area of a triangle ABC, in square inches?

A. 80
B. 45
C. 40
D. 30
E. 15

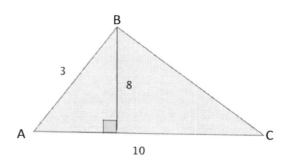

Notes:

Triangles (Area of)

Take 60

What is the area of the triangle ABC below, in square units?

F. 140
G. 112
H. 70
J. 56
K. 24

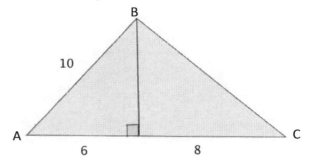

Answer: J

Triangles (Triangle Inequality Theorems)

Which of the following are true, for triangle ABC? [Note: the figure is not drawn to scale]

I.   The length of AB is less than the length of CD?

II.   The length of AB is greater than the length of BD?

III.   The length of BD is less than the length of CD?

        F.   I only

        G.   II only

        H.   III only

        J.   II and III only

        K.   I, II, and III

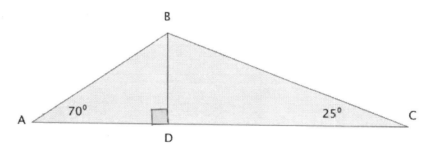

Notes:

▰▰▰▰ SELF-ASSESSMENT ZONE ▰▰▰▰		
CORRECT	**INCORRECT**	**REVIEW THE TIDBIT**
☐ Lucky Guess	☐ Simple Mistake	
☐ Knew It	☐ Need Practice	

Do not turn the page until you are ready to proceed with the timed Take problem

STOP

Triangles (Triangle Inequality Theorems)

Take 60

Which of the following lists the side lengths of Triangle ABC from longest to shortest?

A. AB, BC, AC
B. AB, AC, BC
C. BC, AC, AB
D. AC, BC, AB
E. AC, AB, BC

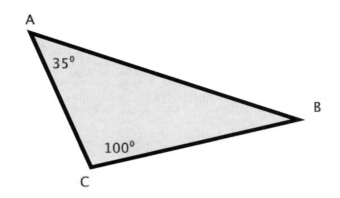

▨▨▨▨ SELF-ASSESSMENT ZONE ▨▨▨▨		
CORRECT	**INCORRECT**	**REVIEW THE TAKE**
☐ Lucky Guess	☐ Simple Mistake	
☐ Knew It	☐ Need Practice	

Answer: B

Triangles (Triangle Inequality Theorems part 2)

Which of the following is a possible side length of AB?

A. 3
B. 4
C. 10
D. 18
E. 20

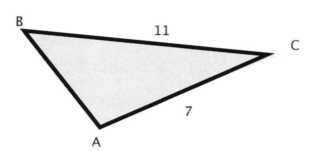

Notes:

CORRECT	**INCORRECT**	**REVIEW THE TIDBIT**
☐ Lucky Guess	☐ Simple Mistake	
☐ Knew It	☐ Need Practice	

Do not turn the page until you are ready to proceed with the timed Take problem

Triangles (Triangle Inequality Theorems Part 2)

Take 60

Which of the following is a possible side length of EF?

    F. 4
    G. 5
    H. 20
    J. 23
    K. 25

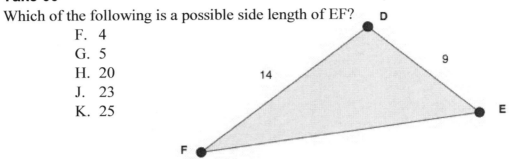

▨▨▨▨ SELF-ASSESSMENT ZONE ▨▨▨▨		
CORRECT	**INCORRECT**	**REVIEW THE TAKE**
□ Lucky Guess	□ Simple Mistake	
□ Knew It	□ Need Practice	

Answer: H

Triangles (Angles)

In the figure below angle DFE = 60 degrees, angle FDE = 80 degrees. Points F, E and G are collinear. What is the measure of angle DEG?

A. 60°
B. 80°
C. 100°
D. 120°
E. 140°

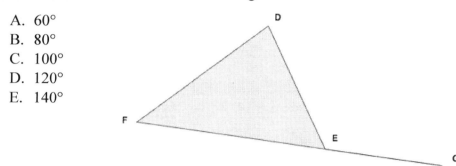

Notes:

▨▨▨ SELF-ASSESSMENT ZONE ▨▨▨		
CORRECT	**INCORRECT**	**REVIEW THE TIDBIT**
□ Lucky Guess	□ Simple Mistake	
□ Knew It	□ Need Practice	

Do not turn the page until you are ready to proceed with the timed Take problem

Triangles (Angles)

Take 50

In the figure below angle ABC = 75 degrees. Triangle ABC is isosceles, AB = BC. Points B, C and D are collinear. What is the measure of angle ACD?

F. 30°
G. 60°
H. 75°
J. 105°
K. 150°

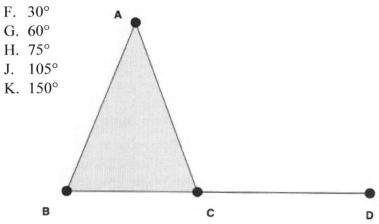

 SELF-ASSESSMENT ZONE 		
CORRECT	**INCORRECT**	**REVIEW THE TAKE**
☐ Lucky Guess	☐ Simple Mistake	
☐ Knew It	☐ Need Practice	

Answer: J

Triangles (Similarities)

The lengths of the corresponding sides of 2 similar right triangles are in a ratio of 3:4. If the hypotenuse of the larger triangle is 10 inches long, how many inches long is the hypotenuse of the smaller triangle?

     A. 3
     B. 5
     C. 7.5
     D. 10.5
     E. 13.3

Notes:

///// SELF-ASSESSMENT ZONE /////		
CORRECT	**INCORRECT**	**REVIEW THE TIDBIT**
☐ Lucky Guess	☐ Simple Mistake	
☐ Knew It	☐ Need Practice	

Do not turn the page until you are ready to proceed with the timed Take problem

Triangles (Similarities)

Take 50

The lengths of the corresponding sides of 2 similar right triangles are in a ratio of 3:5. If the hypotenuse of the smaller triangle is 8 inches long, how many inches long is the hypotenuse of the larger triangle?

    F. 3
    G. 4.8
    H. 7.5
    J. 8
    K. 13.3

▨ SELF-ASSESSMENT ZONE ▨		
CORRECT	**INCORRECT**	**REVIEW THE TAKE**
☐ Lucky Guess	☐ Simple Mistake	
☐ Knew It	☐ Need Practice	

Answer: K

Take Quiz 12: Triangles
Page 204

Polygons (Perimeter)

The perimeter of a parallelogram is 64 inches, and 1 side measures 9 inches. What are the lengths, in inches, of the other 3 sides?

A. 9, 9, 57
B. 9, 21, 21
C. 9, 23, 23
D. 9, 28, 28,
E. Cannot be determined from the given information

Notes:

///// SELF-ASSESSMENT ZONE /////		
CORRECT	**INCORRECT**	**REVIEW THE TIDBIT**
□ Lucky Guess	□ Simple Mistake	
□ Knew It	□ Need Practice	

Do not turn the page until you are ready to proceed with the timed Take problem

Polygons (Perimeter)

Take 50

The perimeter of a rectangle is 72 inches. Its length is twice its width. What are the dimensions of the rectangle?

     F. 8, 16
     G. 12, 24
     H. 14, 28
     J. 16, 32
     K. Cannot be determined from the given information

Answer: G

Polygons (Interior Angles Sum)

What is the measure of each interior angle of this regular polygon?

A. 30°
B. 60°
C. 90°
D. 120°
E. 150°

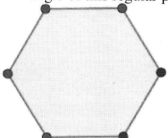

Notes:

////// SELF-ASSESSMENT ZONE //////		
CORRECT	**INCORRECT**	**REVIEW THE TIDBIT**
□ Lucky Guess	□ Simple Mistake	
□ Knew It	□ Need Practice	

Do not turn the page until you are ready to proceed with the timed Take problem

Polygons (Interior Angles Sum)

Take 60

What is the measure of Angle BCD?

  F. 67°
  G. 70°
  H. 73°
  J. 75°
  K. 77°

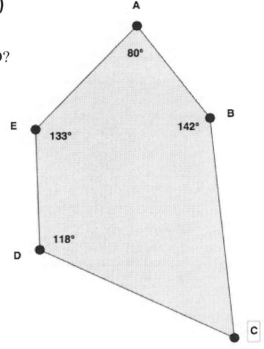

////// SELF-ASSESSMENT ZONE //////		
CORRECT	**INCORRECT**	**REVIEW THE TAKE**
□ Lucky Guess	□ Simple Mistake	
□ Knew It	□ Need Practice	

Answer: F

Polygons (Area)

In the figure below, ABCD is a square. E, F, G and H are midpoints of the sides of square ABCD. What is the ratio of the area of square ABCD to the area of polygon EFGH?

A. 1:3
B. 1:2
C. 3:4
D. 1:1
E. 2:1

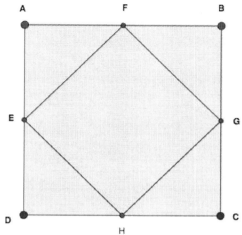

Notes:

Do not turn the page until you are ready to proceed with the timed Take problem

Polygons (Area)

Take 60

In the figure below, ABCD is a square. Points are chosen on each pair of adjacent sides of ABCD to form 4 congruent right triangles, as shown below. Each of these has one leg that is 3 times as long as the other leg. What fraction of square ABCD is polygon EFGH?

F. 4/5
G. 5/4
H. 8/5
J. 9/5
K. 12/5

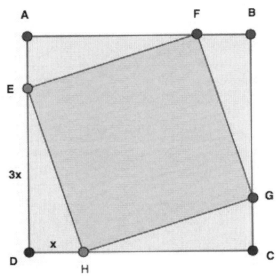

Answer: H

Circles (Area of a Circle)

In the circle below, U is the center and lies on $\overline{BG}$ and $\overline{MT}$. Angle BUM is 51°. Which of the following statements is not true?

A. $\angle TGU = 64.5°$
B. $\overline{BM}$ is parallel to $\overline{TG}$
C. Arc $TAG = 51°$
D. $\overline{TG} \cong \overline{MB}$
E. $\overline{TG} \cong \overline{UG}$

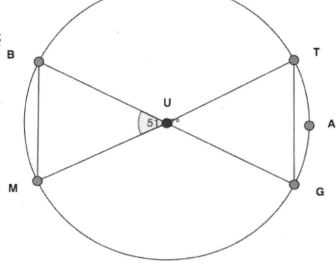

Notes:

▨▨▨ SELF-ASSESSMENT ZONE ▨▨▨		
CORRECT	**INCORRECT**	**REVIEW THE TIDBIT**
☐ Lucky Guess	☐ Simple Mistake	
☐ Knew It	☐ Need Practice	

Do not turn the page until you are ready to proceed with the timed Take problem

137

Circles (Area of a Circle)

Take 60

In the circle below, A is the center and lies on $\overleftrightarrow{CT}$. Which of the following statements is not true? (Diagram not drawn to scale)

F. Arc $ON = 40°$
G. Arc $NC = 65°$
H. Arc $TO = 70°$
J. Arc $TON = 110°$
K. $\overline{AC} \cong \overline{AO}$

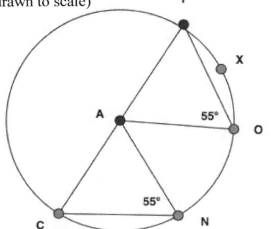

///// SELF-ASSESSMENT ZONE /////		
CORRECT	**INCORRECT**	**REVIEW THE TAKE**
□ Lucky Guess	□ Simple Mistake	
□ Knew It	□ Need Practice	

Answer: G

Take Quiz 13: Polygons
Page 208

Congratulations!

You finished advanced course, class one!

You only learn from experience, so as much as someone can tell you things, you have to go out there and make your own mistakes in order to learn.

— Emma Watson

Advanced Course

Class two

- SOH CAH TOA
- Law of sines and cosines
- Even Functions
- Probability

Straight up on SOH CAH TOA

What is sin A?

A. $\dfrac{5\sqrt{11}}{11}$

B. $\dfrac{5\sqrt{14}}{14}$

C. $\dfrac{\sqrt{154}}{11}$

D. $\dfrac{\sqrt{14}}{5}$

E. $\dfrac{\sqrt{11}}{5}$

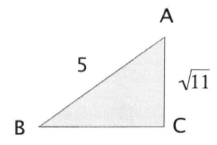

Notes:

		
CORRECT	**INCORRECT**	**REVIEW THE TIDBIT**
☐ Lucky Guess	☐ Simple Mistake	
☐ Knew It	☐ Need Practice	

Do not turn the page until you are ready to proceed with the timed Take problem

Straight up on SOH CAH TOA

Take 60
What is the $\cos \vartheta$?

F. $\dfrac{5}{13}$

G. $\dfrac{5}{12}$

H. $\dfrac{12}{13}$

J. $\dfrac{12}{5}$

K. $\dfrac{13}{5}$

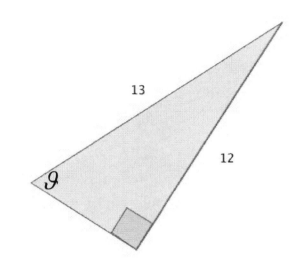

⧄⧄⧄⧄ SELF-ASSESSMENT ZONE ⧄⧄⧄⧄		
CORRECT	**INCORRECT**	**REVIEW THE TAKE**
☐ Lucky Guess	☐ Simple Mistake	
☐ Knew It	☐ Need Practice	

Answer: F

Solving with SOH CAH TOA

What is the expression for the length of $\overline{CD}$?

F. $\dfrac{\tan 35^\circ}{8}$

G. $\dfrac{8}{\tan 35^\circ}$

H. $8 \tan 35^\circ$

J. $\dfrac{1}{8 \bullet \tan 35^\circ}$

K. $\tan(8 \bullet 35^\circ)$

Notes:

▨▨▨ SELF-ASSESSMENT ZONE ▨▨▨		
CORRECT	**INCORRECT**	**REVIEW THE TIDBIT**
☐ Lucky Guess	☐ Simple Mistake	
☐ Knew It	☐ Need Practice	

Do not turn the page until you are ready to proceed with the timed Take problem

STOP

Solving with SOH CAH TOA

Take 60

If $m\angle ABD = 97°$, $AB = 17$ and $m\angle CBD = 32°$, what is the expression for the length of AC ?

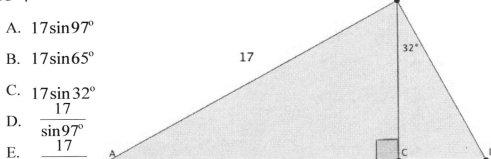

A. $17\sin 97°$

B. $17\sin 65°$

C. $17\sin 32°$

D. $\dfrac{17}{\sin 97°}$

E. $\dfrac{17}{\sin 65°}$

Answer: B

Solving with SOH CAH TOA (Given a Trig Ratio)

If sin A = .4 and AB = 30, what is the length of $\overline{AC}$?

A. 12

B. 10

C. $8\sqrt{21}$

D. $6\sqrt{21}$

E. $\sqrt{21}$

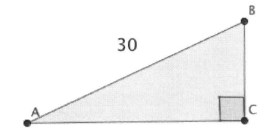

Notes:

Do not turn the page until you are ready to proceed with the timed Take problem

STOP

Solving with SOH CAH TOA (Given a Trig Ratio)

Take 70

If $\cos\theta = .5$ and AB = 3, find the length of $\overline{BC}$.

F. 5

G. 6

H. $3\sqrt{3}$

J. $3\sqrt{5}$

K. 27

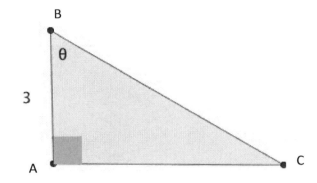

▟▟▟▟ SELF-ASSESSMENT ZONE ▟▟▟▟		
CORRECT	**INCORRECT**	**REVIEW THE TAKE**
☐ Lucky Guess	☐ Simple Mistake	
☐ Knew It	☐ Need Practice	

Answer: H

Solving with SOH CAH TOA (Applied Trig)

Two of your friends went for a ride in a hot air balloon while you stayed behind to do a little mathematical exploration. You are standing at Point A and measure the angle of elevation to the hot air balloon to be 27°. If the horizontal distance between you and the hot air balloon is 300 ft., how high are your two friends, to the nearest foot?

F. 136
G. 144
H. 153
J. 267
K. 589

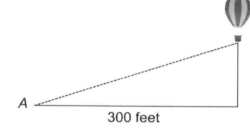

A ⟍ 300 feet

Notes:

Solving with SOH CAH TOA (Applied Trig)

Take 60

Which are curious how high you can reach up the side of your house with your new 20 ft. ladder. If the angle of elevation from the ground to the ladder is 50°, how high up your house can the ladder reach, to the nearest foot?

A. 13
B. 15
C. 17
D. 19
E. 26

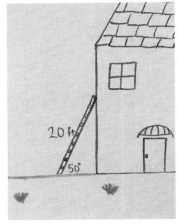

▨▨▨ SELF-ASSESSMENT ZONE ▨▨▨		
CORRECT	**INCORRECT**	**REVIEW THE TAKE**
□ Lucky Guess	□ Simple Mistake	
□ Knew It	□ Need Practice	

Answer: B

Law of Sines and Cosines (Law of Sines)

What is the expression for the length of $\overline{BC}$.

(Note: The Law of Sines states that, for any triangle, the ratios of the sine of an angle to the opposite side are equal).

A. $\dfrac{18\sin 21°}{\sin 97°}$

B. $\dfrac{18\sin 97°}{\sin 21°}$

C. $\dfrac{\sin 21°}{18\sin 97°}$

D. $\dfrac{\sin 97°}{18\sin 21°}$

E. $\dfrac{\sin 21° \sin 97°}{18}$

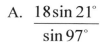

Notes:

///// SELF-ASSESSMENT ZONE /////		
CORRECT	**INCORRECT**	**REVIEW THE TIDBIT**
□ Lucky Guess	□ Simple Mistake	
□ Knew It	□ Need Practice	

Do not turn the page until you are ready to proceed with the timed Take problem

Law of Sines and Cosines (Law of Sines)

Take 60

What is the expression for the length of $\overline{PR}$?

(Note: The Law of Sines states that for any triangle ABC, $\dfrac{\sin A}{a} = \dfrac{\sin B}{b} = \dfrac{\sin C}{c}$)

F. $\dfrac{10\sin 58^{o}}{\sin 33^{o}}$

G. $\dfrac{10\sin 33^{o}}{\sin 58^{o}}$

H. $\dfrac{10}{\sin 58^{o}\sin 33^{o}}$

J. $\dfrac{\sin 58^{\circ}}{10\sin 33^{\circ}}$

K. $\dfrac{\sin 33^{o}}{10\sin 58^{o}}$

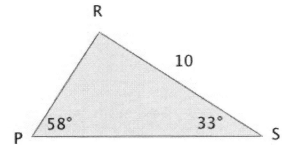

SELF-ASSESSMENT ZONE		
CORRECT	**INCORRECT**	**REVIEW THE TAKE**
□ Lucky Guess	□ Simple Mistake	
□ Knew It	□ Need Practice	

Answer: G

Law of Sines and Cosines (Law of Cosines)

What is the length of $\overline{AB}$ to the nearest foot?
(Note: For any triangle ABC, where A is the side opposite of $\angle A$, B is the side opposite of $\angle B$ and C is the side opposite $\angle C$ the Law of Cosines states $c^2 = a^2 + b^2 - 2ab\cos C$)

A. 219
B. 233
C. 318
D. 386
E. 398

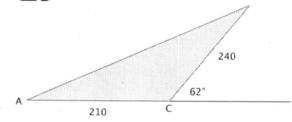

Notes:

Law of Sines and Cosines (Law of Cosines)

Take 80

The distance from Salt Lake City, UT, to Cheyenne, WY, is 440 miles, and from Cheyenne to Rapid City, SD, is 290 miles. Approximately how many miles would a direct trip from Salt Lake City to Rapid City be?

A. 384
B. 526
C. 651
D. 682
E. 713

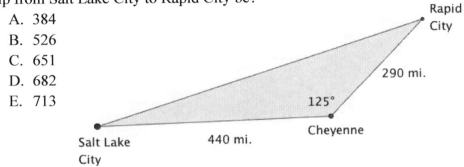

▨▨▨▨	SELF-ASSESSMENT ZONE	▨▨▨▨
CORRECT	**INCORRECT**	**REVIEW THE TAKE**
☐ Lucky Guess	☐ Simple Mistake	
☐ Knew It	☐ Need Practice	

Answer: C

Even Functions

To the right is the graph of $f(x) = 2\cos x$.

Which of the following shows the graph of $g(x) = f(-x)$?

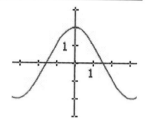

A.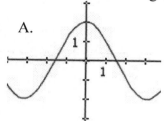

B.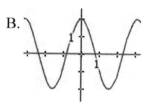

C.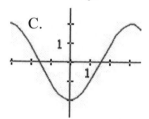

D.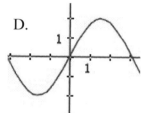

E.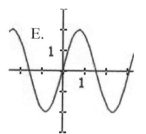

Notes:

	SELF-ASSESSMENT ZONE	
CORRECT	**INCORRECT**	**REVIEW THE TIDBIT**
☐ Lucky Guess	☐ Simple Mistake	
☐ Knew It	☐ Need Practice	

Do not turn the page until you are ready to proceed with the timed Take problem

Even Functions

Take 40

To the right is the graph of $f(x) = \dfrac{1}{3}x^2$.

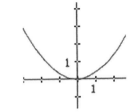

Which of the following shows the graph of $g(x) = f(-x)$?

F.

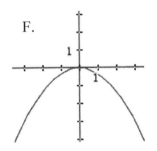

G.

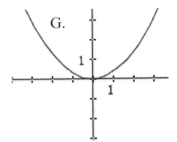

H.

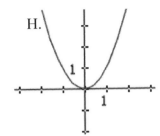

J.

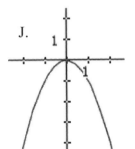

K.

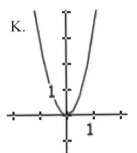

▨▨▨ SELF-ASSESSMENT ZONE ▨▨▨		
CORRECT	**INCORRECT**	**REVIEW THE TAKE**
☐ Lucky Guess	☐ Simple Mistake	
☐ Knew It	☐ Need Practice	

Answer: G

Take Quiz 14: Trigonometry

Page 212

154

Probability

A bag is filled with 7 red marbles, 8 blue marbles, 8 green marbles and 10 yellow marbles. If you reach in and randomly choose one marble, what is the probability the marble will **<u>NOT</u>** be yellow?

- A. .28
- B. .32
- C. .40
- D. .60
- E. .70

Notes:

▨▨▨▨ SELF-ASSESSMENT ZONE ▨▨▨▨		
CORRECT	**INCORRECT**	**REVIEW THE TIDBIT**
□ Lucky Guess	□ Simple Mistake	
□ Knew It	□ Need Practice	

Do not turn the page until you are ready to proceed with the timed Take problem

Probability

Take 40

Daniel has 100 books, 70 of which he has read. If Daniel selects a book at random, what is the probability he has not read it?

      F. 0.3
      G. 0.7
      H. .75
      J. 1.3
      K. 1.7

///// SELF-ASSESSMENT ZONE /////		
CORRECT	**INCORRECT**	**REVIEW THE TAKE**
☐ Lucky Guess	☐ Simple Mistake	
☐ Knew It	☐ Need Practice	

Answer: F

Take Quiz 15: Probability
Page 216

Congratulations!

You completed the advanced course!

Mathematics knows no races or geographic boundaries; for mathematics, the cultural world is one country

— David Hilbert

This page intentionally left blank

Quizzes

QUIZ 1: Inequalities and Equations

7 Minutes—7 Questions

1. Which of the following is equivalent to the inequality $6x - 10 > 4x + 2$?
   - A. $x < -4$
   - B. $x > -4$
   - C. $x > 2$
   - D. $x < 6$
   - E. $x > 6$

2. If $5x + 2 = 13$, then $x =$?
   - F. $\frac{5}{11}$
   - G. $\frac{11}{5}$
   - H. 3
   - J. $\frac{22}{5}$
   - K. 11

3. $|3(-2) - 5(4)| =$?
   - A. -26
   - B. -14
   - C. 14
   - D. 25
   - E. 26

4. Which of the following is equivalent to the inequality $2(3x - 3) < 3(7x + 8)$?
   - F. $x < -2$
   - G. $x > -2$
   - H. $x < -\frac{11}{5}$
   - J. $x > -\frac{11}{5}$
   - K. $x < \frac{10}{9}$

5. $|6 - 2| - |2 - 6| =$?
   - A. -8
   - B. -6
   - C. -4
   - D. 0
   - E. 8

6. Which of the following is equivalent to the inequality $4x - 8 > 8x + 16$?
   - F. $x < -6$
   - G. $x > -6$
   - H. $x < -2$
   - J. $x > 2$
   - K. $x < 6$

160

7. If $7x - 3 = 25$, then $2x = ?$

   A. $\frac{22}{7}$

   B. 4

   C. 8

   D. 16

   E. 28

Do not go on until you are ready to check your answers

Question	Answer	Correct?	Lucky Guess	Knew It	Simple Mistake	Need Practice
SELF-ASSESSMENT ZONE						
1	E	☐	☐	☐	☐	☐
2	G	☐	☐	☐	☐	☐
3	E	☐	☐	☐	☐	☐
4	G	☐	☐	☐	☐	☐
5	D	☐	☐	☐	☐	☐
6	F	☐	☐	☐	☐	☐
7	C	☐	☐	☐	☐	☐
Total		/7				

What do you think is going well so far?

What do you need to do in order to improve?

It's all fun and games until someone divides by zero

— Unknown

Do not go on to the next quiz yet

$2(2x+11)-5(3x-2)$
$(4x+11)-15x+10$
$-11x+21$

$3a^2 - 19a + 1 - 81a + a^2$

QUIZ 2: Polynomials

6 Minutes—6 Questions

1. Which of the following is an equivalent simplified expression for $2(2x + 11) - 5(3x - 2)$?

A. $19x + 32$
B. $-11x + 32$ $4x + 22 - 15x + 10$
C. $-11x + 20$ $-11x + 32$
D. $-11x + 12$
E. $-11x + 9$

2. $(4x^2)^3$ is equivalent to which of the following?

F. $64x^6$ $4x^6$
G. $64x^5$
H. $12x^6$ 64
J. $12x^5$
K. $4x^6$

3. For all x, $(3x + 5)^2 = ?$

A. $6x + 10$ $(3x+5)(3x+5)$
B. $6x^2 + 10$
C. $9x^2 + 25$
D. $9x^2 + 15x + 25$
E. $9x^2 + 30x + 25$ $3x \quad +5$

	$3x$	$15x$
$3x$	$9x^2$	$15x$
$+5$	$15x$	25

$9x^2 + 30x$

4. $3a^2 - 19a + 1 - 81a + a^2$ is equivalent to:

F. $3a^4 - 100a + 1$
G. $4a^2 - 100a + 1$ $-100a$
H. $4a^2 - 62a + 1$
J. $4a^2 - 99a$
K. $3a^2 - 100a + 1$

5. The product $(11x^2y^5)(2x^3y^3)$ is equivalent to:

A. $13x^5y^8$ $22x^6 + y^{15}$
B. $13x^6y^{15}$
C. $22x^5y^8$
D. $22x^6y^{15}$
E. $22x^8y^{125}$

6. The expression $-3x^4(2x^6 - 7x^2)$ is equivalent to:

F. $-6x^{10} + 21x^6$
G. $-6x^{24} + 21x^8$
H. $-6x^{10} - 21x^6$
J. $-6x^{24} - 21x^8$
K. $15x^4$

$-3x^4(2x^6 - 7x^2)$
$-6x^{24} + 21x^8$

$11x^2 \qquad y^5$

	$11x^2$	y^5
$2x^3$	$22x^6$	
y^3	$11xy^2$	

Do not go on until you are ready to check your answers

Question	Answer	Correct?	Lucky Guess	Knew It	Simple Mistake	Need Practice
SELF-ASSESSMENT ZONE						
1	B	☐	☐	☐	☐	☐
2	F	☐	☐	☐	☐	☐
3	E	☐	☐	☐	☐	☐
4	G	☐	☐	☐	☐	☐
5	C	☐	☐	☐	☐	☐
6	F	☐	☐	☐	☐	☐
Total		**/6**				

What do you think is going well so far?

What do you need to do in order to improve?

166

It is not enough to have a good mind. The main thing is to use it well.

— Rene Descartes

Do not go on to the next quiz yet

QUIZ 3: Proportions and Percentages

6 Minutes—6 Questions

1. An architect is drawing the blueprint to a building, with the scale 1.5 cm = 15 ft. If she made the height of the building 16 cm, what will the actual building's height be, in feet?

   A. 360
   B. 240
   C. 160
   D. 150
   E. 140

2. Your favorite store is having a 25% off sale. How much will a $14.95 shirt and $24.99 pair of shorts cost, before tax?

   F. $9.99
   G. $18.74
   H. $24.99
   J. $29.96
   K. $31.95

3. A number is increased by 32%, and the result is 330. What is the number?

   232

   A. 106
   B. 230
   C. 232
   D. 250
   E. 298

4. A tree appears 15 inches tall on a 52" flat screen. How man inches tall does that same tree appear on a 40" flat screen?

   F. 3.4
   G. 10.8
   H. 11.5
   J. 12.1
   K. 19.5

5. A number is increased by 30%. The resulting number is then decreased by 20%. The final number is what percent of the original number?

   A. 90 %
   B. 104 %
   C. 110 %
   D. 117 %
   E. 130 %

6. A number is decreased by 85%, and the result is 9. What is the number?

   F. 60
   G. 62
   H. 68.5
   J. 71.5
   K. 76.5

168

Do not go on until you are ready to check your answers

Question	Answer	Correct?	Lucky Guess	Knew It	Simple Mistake	Need Practice
1	C	☐	☐	☐	☐	☐
2	J	☐	☐	☐	☐	☐
3	D	☐	☐	☐	☐	☐
4	H	☐	☐	☐	☐	☐
5	B	☐	☐	☐	☐	☐
6	F	☐	☐	☐	☐	☐
Total		/6				

SELF-ASSESSMENT ZONE

What do you think is going well so far?

What do you need to do in order to improve?

Education is the most powerful weapon which you can use to change the world

— Nelson Mandela

Do not go on to the next quiz yet

1,2,3,45

QUIZ 4: Averages

4 Minutes—4 Questions

1. To determine a student's overall grade, Mr. Bell throws out the lowest test score and takes the average of the remaining scores. Monica earned the following test scores: 90, 84, 79, 85, 89, and 91. What grade did Monica earn in Mr. Bell's class?

A. 86.0

B. 86.3

C. 86.7

D. 87.3

E. 87.8

79, 84, 85, 89 90, 91

2. What is the median of the following 7 scores?

31, 24, 52, 17, 31, 62, 49

F. 17

G. 31

H. 34.5

J. 40

K. 62

17, 24 31, 31, 49 52, 62

3. To increase the mean of 5 numbers by 3, by how much does the sum of those 5 numbers need to increase?

A. 3

B. 9

C. 10

D. 15

E. 25

4. On a bowling league, two players bowled a 187, three players bowled a 203, and one bowled a 210. What was the league's average score?

F. 187.0

G. 198.8

H. 200.0

J. 201.6

K. 203.0

187, 187, 203, 203, 203, 210

187, 187, 203, 203, 203, 210

172

Do not go on until you are ready to check your answers

Question	Answer	Correct?	Lucky Guess	Knew It	Simple Mistake	Need Practice
		SELF-ASSESSMENT ZONE				
1	E	☐	☐	☐	☐	☐
2	G	☐	☐	☐	☐	☐
3	D	☐	☐	☐	☐	☐
4	G	☐	☐	☐	☐	☐
Total		/4				

What do you think is going well so far?

What do you need to do in order to improve?

It's not that I'm so smart, it's just that I stay with problems longer.

– Albert Einstein

Do not go on to the next quiz yet

STOP

Handwritten at top: S= 30.3952

QUIZ 5: Modeling and Formulas

7 Minutes—7 Questions

1. For the Love of Music Records is having a 25% off sale for all vintage records. If a vintage record costs d dollars, what is the expression for the sale price of the vintage record?

   A. $.25d$ *(circled)* — *handwritten: .25d*
   B. $d - .25$
   C. $d - .25d$ *(circled)*
   D. $d - 25d$
   E. $d - 25$

2. Mobile Cellphone Company is offering a plan for new customers. They charge a monthly fee of $24.99 plus $3.00 for each gigabyte of data usage. Which of the following expressions could be used to model the total monthly cost for a new customer using g gigabytes of data?

   F. $\$24.99g + 3$
   G. $\$27.99g$
   H. $\$21.99g$
   J. $\$30.99g$
   K. $\$24.99 + 3g$ *(circled)*

   handwritten: 2

3. The formula for surface area S of a cylinder is given by the formula $S = 2\pi r^2 + 2\pi rh$, where r is the radius of the circle and h is the height of the cylinder. What is the surface area of the cylinder below, rounded to the nearest square centimeter?

   A. 260
   B. 226
   C. 100 *(circled)*
   D. 97
   E. 83

   Cylinder labeled 2.2 cm (radius) and 5.0 cm (height)

   handwritten: X = 2π 2.2² + 2π(2.2)5.0
   11.12 + 17.28

4. Friday night, Firestone High School is hosting Kenmore High School for a football game. Football tickets cost $6.00 for adults and $2.00 for students. Which of the following expressions represents the total revenue in ticket sales for a adults and c students for Friday night's game?

   F. $6(a + c) + 2c$
   G. $6(a + c)$
   H. $8(a + c)$
   J. $6a + 2c$ *(circled)*
   K. $6c + 2a$

5. Briana Johnson has decided to start a business to manufacture electric cars. In order to start her venture, she must invent $12 million in an automobile production facility. The cost to produce each car will be $14,000, and the selling price will be $30,000. Accounting for her investment in the production facility, which of the following expressions represents the profit, in dollars, that Briana will realize when c cars are produced and sold?

A. $11,663,000c$

B. $30,000c$

C. $16,000c$

D. $44,000c - 12,000,000$

E. $16,000c - 12,000,000$

6. Which of the following mathematical expressions is equivalent to the verbal expression, "5 less than the product of 2 and x is 17"?

F. $5 - 2x = 17$

G. $5 - x^2 = 17$

H. $5 - 2x^2 = 17$

J. $2x - 5 = 17$

K. $x^2 - 5 = 17$

7. The formula $A = P(1 + r)^t$ gives the amount of money in an account where P represents the initial deposit and r is the annually compounded interest rate over t years.

Shay opened a savings account which has an interest rate of 1% compounded annually. If Shay makes an initial deposit of $3,000, which expression represents the amount of money in her account two years from now?

A. $3,000(1.1)^2$

B. $3,000(1.01)^2$

C. $3,000(2)^2$

D. $(3,000 \times 1.01)^2$

E. $(3,000 \times 1.1)^2$

Do not go on until you are ready to check your answers

STOP

177

Question	Answer	Correct?	Lucky Guess	Knew It	Simple Mistake	Need Practice
1	C	☐	☐	☐	☐	☐
2	K	☐	☐	☐	☐	☐
3	C	☐	☐	☐	☐	☐
4	J	☐	☐	☐	☐	☐
5	E	☐	☐	☐	☐	☐
6	J	☐	☐	☐	☐	☐
7	B	☐	☐	☐	☐	☐
Total		/7				

SELF-ASSESSMENT ZONE

What do you think is going well so far?

What do you need to do in order to improve?

Get an education. The one thing that nobody can take away from you is your education. I'm here, I'm present, I'm a contributor to society, I deserve to be part of this conversation, I have an opinion, listen to me roar.

— Gina Rodriguez

Do not go on to the next quiz yet

QUIZ 6: Word Problems

4 Minutes—4 Questions

1. For a youth group party, the youth minister ordered 12 large pizzas. At the end of the party, 9 pizzas had been completely devoured. Half of one pizza remained, $\frac{2}{3}$ of another was left, and just $\frac{1}{4}$ of the last pizza was left. How much pizza was left?

   A. $\frac{4}{9}$

   B. $\frac{11}{12}$

   C. 1

   D. $1\frac{5}{12}$

   E. $1\frac{7}{12}$

2. Kayla earns $9 an hour regular pay as a hostess. For every hour over 40 hours she works each week, she earns 1.5 times her regular pay. If Kayla worked 47 hours last week, how much money did she earn?

   F. $360
   G. $391.50
   H. $423
   J. $450.50
   K. $454.50

3. Senior year, you have quite a few choices of classes! For science, you can either take Botany or Forensics, for social studies, you can choose from Economics, AP US History, or Government, and in math, you can pick from Finite Math, Pre-Calculus, Math Topics, or Discrete Math. How many combinations of science, social studies, and math classes can you take?

   A. 6
   B. 8
   C. 9
   D. 12
   E. 24

4. On Monday, you walked $3\frac{5}{8}$ miles, and on Wednesday, you walked $2\frac{1}{3}$ miles. Thursday, you only walked 1 mile, but on Saturday, you walked $5\frac{3}{4}$ miles. How many miles did you walk over those four days?

F. $11\frac{7}{24}$

G. $11\frac{9}{16}$

H. $12\frac{13}{24}$

J. $12\frac{9}{16}$

K. $12\frac{17}{24}$

Do not go on until you are ready to check your answers

Question	Answer	Correct?	Lucky Guess	Knew It	Simple Mistake	Need Practice
1	D	☐	☐	☐	☐	☐
2	K	☐	☐	☐	☐	☐
3	E	☐	☐	☐	☐	☐
4	K	☐	☐	☐	☐	☐
Total		/4				

SELF-ASSESSMENT ZONE

What do you think is going well so far?

What do you need to do in order to improve?

Don't worry about moving slowly, worry about standing still

— Chinese Proverb

Do not go on to the next quiz yet

QUIZ 7: Linear and Quadratic Functions

8 Minutes—8 Questions

1. Which of the lines below is not parallel to the line
$6x - 2y = 10$

    A. $3x - y = 7$

    B. $-6x + 2y = 20$

    C. $3x + y = 7$

    D. $6x - 2y = 5$

    E. $x - \dfrac{y}{3} = 9$

2. What is the slope of the line that passes through $(-6, -1)$ and $(-4, 2)$?

    F. $-\dfrac{3}{2}$

    G. $\dfrac{3}{10}$

    H. $\dfrac{2}{3}$

    J. $\dfrac{5}{6}$

    K. $\dfrac{3}{2}$

3. All of the graphs have the same scale. Which is the graph of $= -2x + 2$?

A 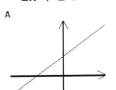 B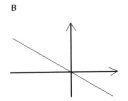

C 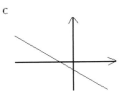 D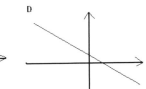

E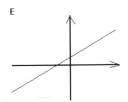

4. What values of x are solutions to $x^2 - 2x = 3$?

    F. -3 and 1

    G. -1 and 3

    H. -2 and -3

    J. -2 and 3

    K. 0 and -3

5. Which of the following is the slope of a line parallel to the line $y = -3x + 7$ in the standard (x, y) coordinate plane?

A. -3

B. $-\dfrac{7}{3}$

C. 3

D. 7

E. 21

6. The slope of the line with the equation $y = bx + d$ is less then the slope of the line with the equation $y = cx + d$. Which of the following statements *must* be true about the relationship between b and c?

F. $b < c$

G. $b > c$

H. $b = c$

J. $b \neq 0$

K. $c = 1$

7. If the line with the equation $y = 2kx - 3$ is perpendicular to the line with the equation $y = \dfrac{1}{2}x + 5$, what is the value of k?

A. -2

B. -1

C. $-\dfrac{1}{2}$

D. 1

E. 2

8. How many solutions are there to the equation

$$x^2 - 5 = 0 ?$$

F. 0

G. 1

H. 2

J. 4

K. 5

Do not go on until you are
ready to check your answers

185

Question	Answer	Correct?	Lucky Guess	Knew It	Simple Mistake	Need Practice
1	C	☐	☐	☐	☐	☐
2	K	☐	☐	☐	☐	☐
3	D	☐	☐	☐	☐	☐
4	G	☐	☐	☐	☐	☐
5	A	☐	☐	☐	☐	☐
6	F	☐	☐	☐	☐	☐
7	B	☐	☐	☐	☐	☐
8	H	☐	☐	☐	☐	☐
Total		/8				

SELF-ASSESSMENT ZONE

What do you think is going well so far?

What do you need to do in order to improve?

Nothing that's worth anything is easy.

— Barack Obama

Do not go on to the next quiz yet

QUIZ 8: All about Coordinates

7 Minutes—7 Questions

1. In the standard *(x, y)* coordinate plane, what is the midpoint of the line segment that has endpoints (-1, 3) and (2, 7) ?

   A. $\left(\frac{1}{2}, 5\right)$

   B. $\left(1, \frac{9}{2}\right)$

   C. $\left(\frac{3}{2}, 2\right)$

   D. $(1, 4)$

   E. $(3, 4)$

2. If point M has a nonzero *x* coordinate and a nonzero *y* coordinate, and the *x* coordinate is nonnegative, in which of 4 quadrants *must* point M be located?

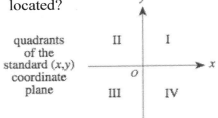

quadrants of the standard *(x,y)* coordinate plane

   F. I only

   G. II only

   H. II or III only

   J. I or IV only

   K. I or II only

3. Find the distance from the point whose coordinates are (4, 3) to the point whose coordinates are (8, 6).

   A. 5

   B. 25

   C. $\sqrt{7}$

   D. $\sqrt{67}$

   E. 15

4. In the standard *(x, y)* coordinate plane, the midpoint of AB is (4, -3), and A is located at (1, -5). If *(x, y)* are the coordinates of B, what is the value of $x + y$?

   F. 19

   G. 8

   H. 6

   J. -1.5

   K. -3

188

5. The sides of a square are 4 mm long. One vertex of the square is at (-4, 0). On a square coordinate grid marked in millimeter units, which of the following points could also be a vertex of the square?

A. (4, 0)

B. (4, 4)

C. (0, 4)

D. (0, -8)

E. (-4, -8)

6. The line $y = -2x + 1$ passes through which of the following quadrants?

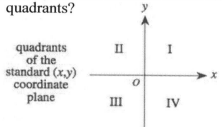

quadrants of the standard (x,y) coordinate plane

F. I and IV only

G. I and II only

H. I, II, and III only

J. I, III, and IV only

K. I, II, and IV only

7. What is the distance between the points (4, 3) and (-1, -2)?

A. $\sqrt{10}$

B. $\sqrt{34}$

C. 7

D. $5\sqrt{2}$

E. 8

Do not go on until you are ready to check your answers

SELF-ASSESSMENT ZONE

Question	Answer	Correct?	Lucky Guess	Knew It	Simple Mistake	Need Practice
1	A	☐	☐	☐	☐	☐
2	J	☐	☐	☐	☐	☐
3	A	☐	☐	☐	☐	☐
4	H	☐	☐	☐	☐	☐
5	C	☐	☐	☐	☐	☐
6	K	☐	☐	☐	☐	☐
7	D	☐	☐	☐	☐	☐
Total		/7				

What do you think is going well so far?

What do you need to do in order to improve?

Some failure in life is inevitable. It is impossible to live without failing at something, unless you live so cautiously that you might as well not have lived at all—in which case, you fail by default

— J. K. Rowling

Do not go on to the next quiz yet

QUIZ 9: Circles and Triangles in the Coordinate Plane

4 Minutes—4 Questions

1. The circle graphed below has center (-5, 3) and is tangent to the y-axis. Which of the following is the equation of the circle?

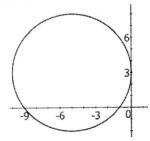

   A. $(x + 5)^2 + (y - 3)^2 = 5$
   B. $(x + 5)^2 + (y - 3)^2 = 25$
   C. $(x - 5)^2 + (y + 3)^2 = 5$
   D. $(x - 5)^2 + (y + 3)^2 = 25$
   E. $(x + 3)^2 + (y - 5)^2 = 25$

2. In the standard (x, y) coordinate plane, the equation of a circle is $(x - 3)^2 + y^2 = 21$. What is the radius and center of this circle?

	radius	center
F.	21	(-3, 0)
G.	$\sqrt{21}$	(-3, 0)
H.	10.5	(3, 0)
J.	$\sqrt{21}$	(3, 0)
K.	21	(3, 0)

For questions 3 and 4, refer to the figure below.

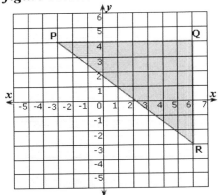

3. What is the area of the triangle PQR, in square units?

   A. 16.5
   B. 31.5
   C. 40.5
   D. 41.5
   E. 63

4. What is the perimeter of triangle PQR?

   F. 130
   G. 146
   H. $\sqrt{130}$
   J. $16 + \sqrt{130}$
   K. $63 + \sqrt{130}$

Do not go on until you are ready to check your answers

Question	Answer	Correct?	Lucky Guess	Knew It	Simple Mistake	Need Practice
1	B	☐	☐	☐	☐	☐
2	J	☐	☐	☐	☐	☐
3	B	☐	☐	☐	☐	☐
4	J	☐	☐	☐	☐	☐
Total		/4				

SELF-ASSESSMENT ZONE

What do you think is going well so far?

What do you need to do in order to improve?

The value of a problem is not so much coming up with the answer as in the ideas and attempted ideas it forces on the would be solver.

— I. N. Herstein

Do not go on to the next quiz yet

QUIZ 10: Logs, Exponents, and Head Scratchers

7 Minutes—7 Questions

1. What is $\log_4 64$?

   A. 2
   B. 3
   C. 4
   D. 16
   E. 60

2. If $x > 0$ and $y \le 0$, then which of the following inequalities must be true?

   F. $|x| < |y|$
   G. $|y| < |x|$
   H. $x + y < 0$
   J. $x - y < 0$
   K. $x - y > 0$

3. If x is a real number and $x < 0$, then which of the following is negative?

   A. $-2x$
   B. x^2
   C. $(-x)^2$
   D. $-x^2$
   E. x^4

4. In the real numbers, what is the solution of the equation $9^{1-x} = 27^{2x+3}$?

   F. $-\frac{1}{4}$
   G. $-\frac{2}{3}$
   H. $-\frac{7}{8}$
   J. $-\frac{8}{7}$
   K. $-\frac{7}{4}$

5. If x and y are real numbers such that $x > 1$ and $y < -1$, then which of the following inequalities must be true?

   A. $\frac{x}{y} > 0$
   B. $\frac{y}{x} > 0$
   C. $xy > 0$
   D. $|xy| > 0$
   E. $|x| - |y| > 0$

6. What is $\log_3 81$?

   F. 2
   G. 3
   H. 4
   J. 9
   K. 27

7. In the real numbers, what is the solution of the equation $4^{x+2} = 8^{x-3}$?

    A. 13

    B. 11

    C. 8

    D. 5

    E. no solution

Do not go on until you are ready to check your answers

STOP

Question	Answer	Correct?	Lucky Guess	Knew It	Simple Mistake	Need Practice
		SELF-ASSESSMENT ZONE				
1	B	☐	☐	☐	☐	☐
2	K	☐	☐	☐	☐	☐
3	D	☐	☐	☐	☐	☐
4	H	☐	☐	☐	☐	☐
5	D	☐	☐	☐	☐	☐
6	H	☐	☐	☐	☐	☐
7	A	☐	☐	☐	☐	☐
Total		/7				

What do you think is going well so far?

What do you need to do in order to improve?

Stay focused, go after your dreams and keep moving toward your goals.

— LL Cool J

Do not go on to the next quiz yet

STOP

QUIZ 11: Substitution

1. A function $f(x)$ is defined as $f(x) = -5x^2$. What is $f(-3)$?

   A. -225
   B. -45
   C. 45
   D. 75
   E. 225

2. Given $f(x) = 4x + 1$ and $g(x) = x^2 - 3$, what is the expression for $f(g(x))$?

   F. $16x^2 - 2$
   G. $16x^2 + 8x - 2$
   H. $4x^2 - 12$
   J. $4x^2 - 11$
   K. $4x^2 - 2$

3. What is the value of the expression $(x - y)^2$ when $x = 3$ and $y = -4$?

   A. -49
   B. -1
   C. 1
   D. 7
   E. 49

4. Given $g(x) = 2x^2 - 3$, what is the value of $g(-1)$?

   F. -7
   G. -5
   H. -1
   J. 1
   K. 5

5. A function P is defined as follows:
   for $x > 0$,
   $$P(x) = x^5 - x^4 - 30x + 30$$
   for $x < 0$,
   $$P(x) = -x^5 - x^4 + 30x + 30$$
   What is (-1) ?

   A. -2
   B. 2
   C. 0
   D. 58
   E. 60

Do not go on until you are ready to check your answers

SELF-ASSESSMENT ZONE

Question	Answer	Correct?	Lucky Guess	Knew It	Simple Mistake	Need Practice
1	B	☐	☐	☐	☐	☐
2	J	☐	☐	☐	☐	☐
3	E	☐	☐	☐	☐	☐
4	H	☐	☐	☐	☐	☐
5	C	☐	☐	☐	☐	☐
Total		/5				

What do you think is going well so far?

What do you need to do in order to improve?

You have to set a goal, and then you have to be focused and disciplined

— Arturo Moreno

Do not go on to the next quiz yet

QUIZ 12: Triangles

5 Minutes—5 Questions

1. For triangle ABC, AC = 3 and
   BC = 4. What is the length of AB?
   A. 4
   B. √24
   C. √34
   D. 6
   E. 34

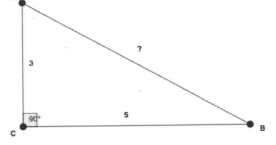

2. For the 30-60-90 triangle DEF,
   ED = 6√3 and EF = 6. What is
   the length of DF?
   F. 6√2
   G. 6√3
   H. 12
   J. 12√3
   K. 6√6

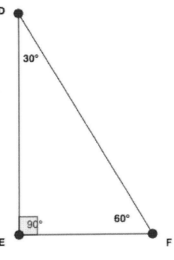

3. For triangle ABC, AC = 5 and
   AB = 13. What is the area of
   triangle ABC in square units?
   A. 25
   B. 30
   C. 32.5
   D. 60
   E. 65

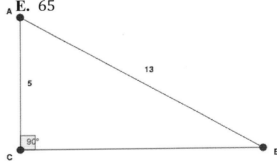

4. If two sides of a triangle are 7 units and 11 units long, which of the following is a possible length of the third side?

    F. 17
    G. 18
    H. 19
    J. 20
    K. 21

5. For triangle DEG, angle DGF = 44°. Which of the following statements are true? (drawing not to scale)

A. $GF < FE$
B. $GF > FE$
C. $GF > DF$
D. $DF < FE$
E. $FE > DE$

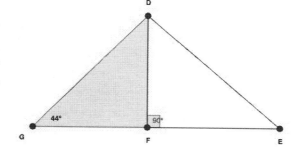

Do not go on until you are ready to check your answers

Question	Answer	Correct?	Lucky Guess	Knew It	Simple Mistake	Need Practice
1	C	☐	☐	☐	☐	☐
2	H	☐	☐	☐	☐	☐
3	B	☐	☐	☐	☐	☐
4	F	☐	☐	☐	☐	☐
5	B	☐	☐	☐	☐	☐
Total		/5				

SELF-ASSESSMENT ZONE

What do you think is going well so far?

What do you need to do in order to improve?

Great success comes only with great ambition

— Jackie Chan

Do not go on to the next quiz yet

QUIZ 13: Polygons and Circles

5 Minutes—5 Questions

1. The perimeter of a parallelogram is 96 inches, and 1 side measures 20 inches. What are the lengths, in inches, of the other 3 sides?

    A. 20, 18, 18
    B. 20, 28, 28
    C. 20, 38, 38
    D. 20, 20, 56
    E. Cannot be determined from the given information

2. What is the measure of each interior angle of this regular polygon?

    F. 108
    G. 120
    H. 135
    J. 140
    K. 150

3. What is the measure of angle HID?

    A. 85
    B. 88
    C. 90
    D. 93
    E. 101

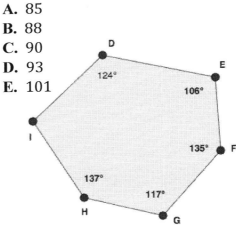

4. The radius of circle G is 6 inches long. Angle DGE is 120°. How many inches long is chord DF?

    F. $3\sqrt{2}$
    G. $3\sqrt{3}$
    H. $6\sqrt{2}$
    J. $6\sqrt{3}$
    K. 12

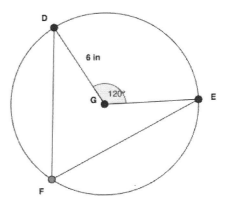

5. For pentagon ABCDE, angles A, C and D are right angles. Segment AB is 24 feet long and segment BC is 25 feet long. What is the area in square feet of the pentagon?

A. 625

B. 625√3

C. 1136.53

D. 913

E. 1350

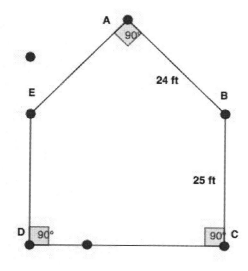

Do not go on until you are
ready to check your answers

209

			SELF-ASSESSMENT ZONE			
Question	Answer	Correct?	Lucky Guess	Knew It	Simple Mistake	Need Practice
1	B	☐	☐	☐	☐	☐
2	H	☐	☐	☐	☐	☐
3	E	☐	☐	☐	☐	☐
4	J	☐	☐	☐	☐	☐
5	C	☐	☐	☐	☐	☐
Total		/5				

What do you think is going well so far?

What do you need to do in order to improve?

You can't be afraid to fail. It's the only way you succeed – you're not gonna succeed all the time, and I know that.

– LeBron James

Do not go on to the next quiz yet

QUIZ 14: Trigonometry

7 Minutes—7 Questions

1. What is C ?

A. $\dfrac{3}{5}$

B. $\dfrac{3}{4}$

C. $\dfrac{4}{5}$

D. $\dfrac{4}{3}$

E. $\dfrac{5}{3}$

2. To approximate the length of a lake, a surveyor starts at one end of the lake and walks 245 yards. He then turns 110° and walks 270 yards until he arrives at the other end of the lake. Approximately how long is the lake, to the nearest yard?

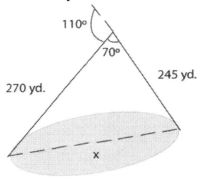

F. 214

G. 288

H. 296

J. 347

K. 365

3. Given $m < ADB = 142°$ and $DC = 12$, which is the expression for the length of AD?

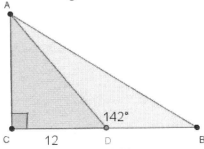

A. $12tan38°$

B. $12tan142°$

C. $\dfrac{tan38}{12}$

D. $\dfrac{12}{tan38°}$

E. *not enough information*

4. Which of the following represents an even function?

F. $f(x) = sin3x$

G. $f(x) = cosx$

H. $f(x) = |x - 2|$

J. $f(x) = x^3$

K. $f(x) = \sqrt{x + 1}$

5. $\sin^2 A + \cos^2 B = ?$

A. 1

B. $\frac{16}{5}$

C. $\frac{32}{5}$

D. $\frac{32}{25}$

E. $\frac{32}{50}$

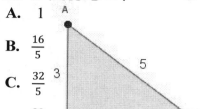

7. If $sinA = .25$ and the length of AB is 30, what is the length of side AC?

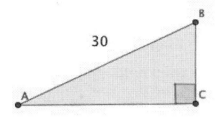

A. 27

B. 28

C. 29

D. 30

E. 31

6. Which of the following is an expression for the length of AB? (The Law of Sines states that $\frac{sinA}{a} = \frac{sinB}{b} = \frac{sinC}{c}$ for any triangle ABC, where a is the side opposite angle A, b is the side opposite angle B, and c is the side opposite angle C)

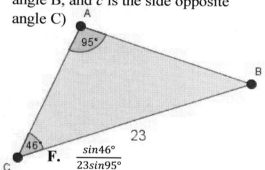

F. $\frac{sin46°}{23sin95°}$

G. $\frac{23}{sin46°sin95°}$

H. $\frac{sin95°}{23sin46°}$

J. $\frac{23sin46°}{sin95°}$

K. $\frac{23sin95°}{sin46°}$

Do not go on until you are ready to check your answers

213

Question	Answer	Correct?	Lucky Guess	Knew It	Simple Mistake	Need Practice
1	B	☐	☐	☐	☐	☐
2	H	☐	☐	☐	☐	☐
3	A	☐	☐	☐	☐	☐
4	G	☐	☐	☐	☐	☐
5	D	☐	☐	☐	☐	☐
6	J	☐	☐	☐	☐	☐
7	C	☐	☐	☐	☐	☐
Total		/7				

SELF-ASSESSMENT ZONE

What do you think is going well so far?

What do you need to do in order to improve?

Math is like going to the gym for your brain. It sharpens your mind.

— Danica McKellar

Do not go on to the next quiz yet

QUIZ 15: Probability

4 Minutes—4 Questions

1. A bag contains 45 red marbles, 20 blue marbles, 15 purple marbles, and 20 orange marbles. If you randomly pick one marble from the bag, what is the probability that it will be either red OR orange?

   A. .20

   B. .25

   C. .45

   D. .35

   E. .65

2. The results of the election are displayed in the table below. Approximately what percentage of the vote did Charles receive?

Candidate	Number of Votes
Ashley	45
Watson	25
Charles	50
Bennett	15

   F. 15%

   G. 37%

   H. 50%

   J. 59%

   K. 75%

3. There are 1000 jelly beans in a jar. If the chance that you will randomly pick a red jelly bean is 22%, what is the chance that you will NOT pick a red jelly bean?

   A. 22%

   B. 38%

   C. 75%

   D. 78%

   E. 88%

4. An integer from 1-100, inclusive, is to be chosen at random. What is the probability that this number will have 8 as at least 1 digit?

   F. $\frac{10}{100}$

   G. $\frac{8}{99}$

   H. $\frac{19}{99}$

   J. $\frac{19}{100}$

   K. $\frac{20}{100}$

216

Do not go on until you are ready to check your answers

Question	Answer	Correct?	Lucky Guess	Knew It	Simple Mistake	Need Practice
1	E	☐	☐	☐	☐	☐
2	G	☐	☐	☐	☐	☐
3	D	☐	☐	☐	☐	☐
4	J	☐	☐	☐	☐	☐
Total		/4				

SELF-ASSESSMENT ZONE

What do you think is going well so far?

What do you need to do in order to improve?

Going to school, reading, and doing our homework wasn't just a way of passing time, it was our future

— Malala Yousafzai

This page intentionally left blank

Homework

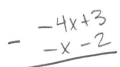

$-4x+3$
$-x-2$

= actual answer

Home Work 1.1.1 — Day After

Directions: Time yourself while answering these questions. Try your best to complete them in ten minutes or less! When you are done, write how long the ten problems actually took you to complete. Check your answers with the key you received, and grade yourself.

1. $|2(-11) + 3(3)| =?$

- A.   -31
- B.   -13
- C.   5
- D.   13
- E.   31

$22+$ $-4x+3$

0.3
0.375

2. Place the fractions in order from least to greatest: $\frac{2}{5}, \frac{3}{8}, \frac{1}{4}, \frac{3}{10}$

- F. $\frac{2}{5}, \frac{1}{4}, \frac{3}{10}, \frac{3}{8}$
- G. $\frac{1}{4}, \frac{3}{8}, \frac{2}{5}, \frac{3}{10}$
- H. $\frac{1}{4}, \frac{3}{10}, \frac{3}{8}, \frac{2}{5}$
- J. $\frac{3}{10}, \frac{3}{8}, \frac{2}{5}, \frac{1}{4}$
- K. $\frac{3}{10}, \frac{3}{8}, \frac{1}{4}, \frac{2}{5}$

$5(x-7)=11$
$5x-35=11$
$5x \quad +35$
$\frac{5x}{5} = \frac{46}{5}$
$x =$

3. If $5(x - 7) = 11$, then $x =?$

- A. $-\frac{46}{5}$
- B. $-\frac{18}{5}$
- C. $-\frac{4}{5}$
- D. $\frac{24}{5}$
- E. $\frac{46}{5}$

4. The expression $(-4x + 3) - (x - 2)$ is equivalent to which of the following expressions?

- F. $-5x + 5$
- G. $-3x + 1$
- H. $-3x + 5$
- J. $4x + 1$
- K. $4x - 5$

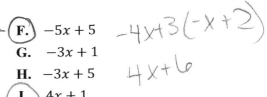

$-4x+3(-x+2)$
$4x+6$

5. Which of the following is equivalent to the inequality $2x + 5 > 5x - 22$?

$2x+5>5x-22$

- A. $x < -9$
- B. $x > -9$
- C. $x > -\frac{27}{7}$
- D. $x < 9$
- E. $x > 9$

$2x+5>5x-22$
$\quad -5 \quad -5x$
$\quad -5x$
$2x > 5x-27$
$-5x$
$-3x > -27$
$x < 9$

6. If $f(x)$ is defined as $f(x) = 5x^2 - 3$, what is $f(-3)$?

- F.   221
- G.   42
- H.   -48
- J.   -42
- K.   -228

$5x^2 -3(-3)$
$5x^2 +9$

$5x^2-3(-3)$
$-15x^2+9$

$5(-3)^2-3$
$-15\cdot3$
$-225-3$
$-3-5(-3)^2-3$
$0=5(-3)^2$

222

[handwritten at top:]
$5(2x-3) < 2(x+4)$
$10x - 15 < 2x + 8$
$+15$
$16x < 2x + 23$

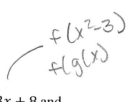
$f(x^2-3)$
$f(g(x))$

7. Which of the following is equivalent
to the inequality
$5(2x - 3) < 2(x + 4)$?

[handwritten:]
$10x - 15 < 2(x+4)$
$10x - 15 < 2x + 8$
-15
$10x < 2x + 3$
$8x = 3/8$
$\frac{8x}{8} = \frac{3}{8}$
$x = 0.375$

A. $x < -\frac{7}{8}$

B. $x > -\frac{7}{8}$

C. $x < \frac{7}{8}$

D. $x > \frac{7}{8}$

E. $x < \frac{23}{8}$

8. The expression
$(4x - 3y^2)(4x + 3y^2)$ is equivalent
to:

[handwritten:] Actual answer

F. $16x^2 - 9y^4$ $\quad 4x - 3y^2$
G. $16x^2 - 6y^4$ $\quad 4x + 3y^2$
H. $16x^2 + 9y^4$ $\quad \overline{}$
J. $8x^2 - 9y^4$ $\quad 8x$
K. $8x^2 - 6y^4$

9. For all x, $(2x - 5)^2 = ?$

A. $4x + 10$
B. $4x^2 + 25$
C. $4x^2 - 10x + 25$
D. $4x^2 - 20x + 25$
E. $4x^2 + 20x + 25$

[handwritten:] FOIL
$(2x-5)(2x-5)$

[handwritten box method:]
	$2x$	-5
$2x$	$4x^2$	$-10x$
-5	$-10x$	25

$4x^2 - 20x + 25$

10. Given $f(x) = 3x + 8$ and
$g(x) = x^2 - 3$, what is the
expression for $f(g(x))$?

F. $x^2 + 3x + 5$
G. $3x^3 + 11x^2 - 9x - 24$
H. $3x^2 - 1$
J. $9x^2 + 48x + 61$
K. $9x^2 + 48x + 64$

[handwritten:]
$3x + 8(x^2 - 3)$
$3x^3 - 24$

[handwritten:]
$10x - 15 < 2x + 8$
$-2x$
$8x - 15 < 8$
$+15$
$\frac{8x}{8} < \frac{23}{8}$
$x = \frac{23}{8}$

223

			SELF-ASSESSMENT ZONE			
Question	Answer	Correct?	Lucky Guess	Knew It	Simple Mistake	Need Practice
1	D	☐	☐	☐	☐	☐
2	H	☐	☐	☐	☐	☐
3	E	☐	☐	☐	☐	☐
4	F	☐	☐	☐	☐	☐
5	D	☐	☐	☐	☐	☐
6	G	☐	☐	☐	☐	☐
7	E	☐	☐	☐	☐	☐
8	F	☐	☐	☐	☐	☐
9	D	☐	☐	☐	☐	☐
10	H	☐	☐	☐	☐	☐
Total		/10				

What do you think is going well so far?

What do you need to do in order to improve?

Review the problems:

Failure is another steppingstone to greatness.

—Oprah Winfrey

Home Work 1.1.2 — So I don't forget

Directions: Time yourself while answering these questions. Try your best to complete them in ten minutes or less! When you are done, write how long the ten problems actually took you to complete. Check your answers with the key you received, and grade yourself.

1. If $4x + 7 = 15$, then $3x = $?

    A.   -2
    B.   2
    C.   6
    D.   8
    E.   12

2. If $x = 7$, $y = 4$, and $z = -5$, what does $(x - y + z)(y - z)$ equal?

    F.   -72
    G.   -18
    H.   -8
    J.   2
    K.   8

3. $g(x)$ is defined as $g(x) = 4x^2$. What is $g(-2)$?

    A.   -64
    B.   -16
    C.   0
    D.   16
    E.   64

4. Which of the following is equivalent to the inequality $-5 > 5x + 30$?

    F. $x < -7$
    G. $x > -7$
    H. $x > -5$
    J. $x < 5$
    K. $x > 5$

5. For all x, $(3x - 2)^2 = $?

    A. $6x + 4$
    B. $6x^2 - 4$
    C. $9x^2 - 12x + 4$
    D. $6x^2 - 12x - 4$
    E. $9x^2 + 4$

6. Given $f(x) = x^2 + 2$ and $g(x) = x - 3$, what is the expression for $f(g(x))$?

    F. $x^2 - 6x + 11$
    G. $x^2 + 6x + 11$
    H. $x^2 - 6x - 4$
    J. $x^2 + 6x - 4$
    K. $x^2 + 11$

7. $|7 - 5| - |7 - 10| = ?$

    A.   -5
    B.   -1
    C.   0
    D.   1
    E.   5

8. The product $(-2x^3y^4)(-3x^2y)$ is equivalent to:

    F. $-6x^6y^4$
    G. $-6x^5y^5$
    H. $5x^5y^5$
    J. $6x^5y^5$
    K. $6x^6y^4$

9. Which of the following is equivalent to the inequality
$-3(4x - 3) < 5(4x - 11)$?

    A. $x < -8$
    B. $x > -8$
    C. $x < 2$
    D. $x > 2$
    E. $x < 8$

10. The expression
$(-5x + 2) - (2x - 3)$ is equivalent to:

    F. $10x^2 - 6$
    G. $10x^2 - 19x - 6$
    H. $-3x + 5$
    J. $-7x + 5$
    K. $3x - 1$

Question	Answer	Correct?	Lucky Guess	Knew It	Simple Mistake	Need Practice
1	C	☐	☐	☐	☐	☐
2	G	☐	☐	☐	☐	☐
3	D	☐	☐	☐	☐	☐
4	F	☐	☐	☐	☐	☐
5	C	☐	☐	☐	☐	☐
6	F	☐	☐	☐	☐	☐
7	B	☐	☐	☐	☐	☐
8	J	☐	☐	☐	☐	☐
9	D	☐	☐	☐	☐	☐
10	J	☐	☐	☐	☐	☐
Total		/10				

SELF-ASSESSMENT ZONE

What do you think is going well so far?

What do you need to do in order to improve?

Review the problems:

Fall seven times, stand up eight.

— Japanese proverb

Home Work 1.2.1 — Day After

1. In order to increase profit, a boutique owner is raising the price of a $24.00 vintage necklace by 15%. What will the new price of the necklace be?

   A. $ 3.60
   B. $ 25.50
   C. $ 26.40
   D. $ 27.60
   E. $ 39.00

2. Your friends ordered 3 pizzas, each with 8 slices. After an hour, five slices of the first pizza were gone, and of the second pizza, 25% remained. Half of the third pizza was eaten. What percentage of one whole pizza remained?

   F. 87.5
   G. 88.8
   H. 100
   J. 112.5
   K. 150

3. Matt earns scores of 88, 90, 86, and 91 on his first four algebra tests of the quarter. What is the lowest score Matt can earn on his fifth test to have a 90 average?

   A. 88
   B. 90
   C. 92
   D. 93
   E. 95

4. The height of a fir oak tree is directly proportional to the length of its shadow, at a given time. Vicky is curious how tall her favorite fir oak tree is, so she measures its shadow to be 59 ft. long. To compare, and at the same time of day, she measures the shadow of a 6 ft. tall fir oak tree to be 10 ft. long. How tall is Vicky's favorite fir oak tree, rounded to the nearest foot?

   F. 34
   G. 35
   H. 36
   J. 63
   K. 98

5. Foot Locker is having a storewide 30% off sale. How much will you pay, before tax, for shoes that are typically priced at $74.00?

   A. $ 22.20
   B. $ 44.00
   C. $ 51.80
   D. $ 71.00
   E. $ 77.00

6. What is the median of the following set of values?

   19, 7, 0, 8, 10, 21, 13

   F. 8
   G. 10
   H. 11.1
   J. 11.5
   K. 13

7. To compute a student's overall grade, Mrs. Crabtree drops the lowest score out of the four quarter grades, the midterm grade, and the final grade, then averages the remaining five scores. Micah earned the following quarter grades: 78, 81, 80, and 84. He earned a 75 on the midterm and an 82 on the final. What is Micah's overall grade?

    A. 80
    B. 80.5
    C. 81
    D. 81.5
    E. 82

8. The following table shows Kentucky basketball scores over seven games. What is the difference between Kentucky's average game score and their opponent's average game score?

Opponent	Opponent's Score	Kentucky's Score
Georgia	64	72
Florida	50	67
Florida	49	64
Auburn	67	91
Arkansas	63	78
Hampton	56	79
Cincinnati	51	64

    F. 23
    G. 21
    H. 17
    J. 13
    K. 11

9. A dish set is on sale for $32 after a 60% discount. What was the set's original price?

    A. $ 92
    B. $ 80
    C. $ 26
    D. $ 19.20
    E. $ 12.80

10. A $100 jersey is on sale for 20% off. If sales tax is 7%, what is the final cost of the jersey?

    F. $ 87.00
    G. $ 85.60
    H. $ 80.07
    J. $ 73.00
    K. $ 67.80

Question	Answer	Correct?	Lucky Guess	Knew It	Simple Mistake	Need Practice
1	D	☐	☐	☐	☐	☐
2	J	☐	☐	☐	☐	☐
3	E	☐	☐	☐	☐	☐
4	G	☐	☐	☐	☐	☐
5	C	☐	☐	☐	☐	☐
6	G	☐	☐	☐	☐	☐
7	C	☐	☐	☐	☐	☐
8	H	☐	☐	☐	☐	☐
9	B	☐	☐	☐	☐	☐
10	G	☐	☐	☐	☐	☐
Total		/10				

SELF-ASSESSMENT ZONE

What do you think is going well so far?

What do you need to do in order to improve?

Review the problems:

The policy of being too cautious is the greatest risk of all.

– Jawaharlal Nehru

Home Work 1.2.2 — So I don't forget

1. A number is increased by 20%, and the result is 168. What is the number?

   A. 140
   B. 148
   C. 152
   D. 160
   E. 201.6

2. An oak tree's height is directly proportional to the length of its shadow. At 3:00 pm, you measure the shadow of an 8 ft. tall oak tree to be 3.5 ft. in length. At the same time of day, you measure another oak tree's shadow to be 13 ft. in length. How tall is the other oak tree, to the nearest tenth of a foot?

   F. 5.7
   G. 17.5
   H. 29.7
   J. 29.8
   K. 30.0

3. It costs Beats by Dre $14 to make a pair of their least expensive headphones, which the company then sells for $200.00. The selling price is what percent of the manufacturing cost?

   A. 1429
   B. 142.9
   C. 78.0
   D. 14.3
   E. 7.0

4. A number is increased by 30%, and the resulting umber is then decreased by 15%. The final number is what percent of the original number?

   F. 101.5
   G. 105
   H. 110.5
   J. 115
   K. 130

5. David's test scores were 76, 82, 84, and 72. What score does David need on his fifth test so that his average will be 80?

   A. 90
   B. 88
   C. 86
   D. 84
   E. 82

6. What is the median of the following data set?

16, 5, 1, 6, 10, 42, 20

F.   6
G.   10
H.   11
J.   13
K.   16

9. In his last eleven games, Lebron James scored 37, 27, 29, 18, 17, 27, 31, 21, 26, 16, and 29 points. What is his average points per game during that stretch?

A.   31
B.   29
C.   27
D.   25
E.   23

7. Jill bowled a 242, 186, 256, and 220. If her league drops her lowest game score when computing her average, what is Jill's average bowling score, according to her league?

A.   239
B.   232
C.   228
D.   226
E.   218

10. A score of 36 out of 40 is what percentage out of 100?

F.   36
G.   72
H.   80
J.   86
K.   90

8. A $155 pair of sunglasses is on sale for 45% off. What is the sale price of the sunglasses?

F. $ 69.75
G. $ 78.52
H. $ 85.25
J. $ 90.00
K. $ 110

Question	Answer	Correct?	Lucky Guess	Knew It	Simple Mistake	Need Practice
1	A	☐	☐	☐	☐	☐
2	H	☐	☐	☐	☐	☐
3	A	☐	☐	☐	☐	☐
4	H	☐	☐	☐	☐	☐
5	C	☐	☐	☐	☐	☐
6	G	☐	☐	☐	☐	☐
7	A	☐	☐	☐	☐	☐
8	H	☐	☐	☐	☐	☐
9	D	☐	☐	☐	☐	☐
10	K	☐	☐	☐	☐	☐
Total		/10				

SELF-ASSESSMENT ZONE

What do you think is going well so far?

What do you need to do in order to improve?

Review the problems:

The question isn't who's going to let me; it's who's going to stop me.

— Ayn Rand

Home Work 2.1.1 — Day After

Directions: Time yourself while answering these questions. Try your best to complete them in ten minutes or less! When you are done, write how long the ten problems actually took you to complete. Check your answers with the key you received, and grade yourself.

1. Lines l and m are parallel. The equation of line l is $y = 5x + 1$, and the equation of line m is $y = 2kx - \frac{1}{3}$. What is the value of k?

   A. $\frac{2}{5}$

   B. 1

   C. 2

   D. $\frac{5}{2}$

   E. 5

2. What is the slope for a line parallel to the line with the equation $y = x + 3$ in the standard (x, y) coordinate plane?

   F. 0

   G. 1

   H. 3

   J. 4

   K. 6

3. What values of x are the solutions to $x^2 - 9x = -20$?

   A. 4 and 5

   B. -4 and -5

   C. 4 and -5

   D. -4 and 5

   E. 0 and 4

4. What is the slope of the line that passes through the points $(4, 5)$ and $(-2, -7)$?

   F. -2

   G. -1

   H. $\frac{1}{2}$

   J. 1

   K. 2

5. If the line with the equation $y = ax + b$ is perpendicular to the line with the equation $y = cx + b$, and $a < 0$, which of the following must be true about c?

   A. $c < 0$

   B. $c = 0$

   C. $c > 0$

   D. $c = 1$

   E. $c = a$

6. The figure below most closely represents the graph of which of the following equations?

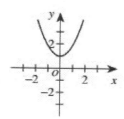

    F. $-x^2 + 1$

    G. $x^2 + 1$

    H. $x^2 - 1$

    J. $2x^2$

    K. $x^3 - 1$

7. Which of the following expressions is the factored form of $x^2 + 2x - 63$?

    A. $(x + 7)(x + 2)$
    B. $(x - 7)(x - 9)$
    C. $(x + 7)(x + 9)$
    D. $(x + 7)(x - 9)$
    E. $(x - 7)(x + 9)$

8. What is the y-intercept of the graph of the line with the equation $-2x + 3y = 6$?

    F. -2

    G. $\frac{2}{3}$

    H. 2

    J. 3

    K. 6

9. Which of the following is the graph of the linear function $(x) = 2x - 1$?

A. 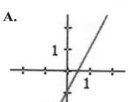   **D.**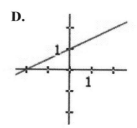

B. 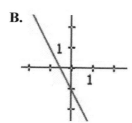   **E.**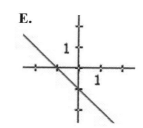

C.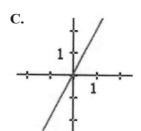

10. Which of the following points lies on the line $x - 2y = 7$?

    F. (11, 4)

    G. (11, 2)

    H. (2, -3)

    J. (1, -4)

    K. (0, -4)

SELF-ASSESSMENT ZONE

Question	Answer	Correct?	Lucky Guess	Knew It	Simple Mistake	Need Practice
1	D	☐	☐	☐	☐	☐
2	G	☐	☐	☐	☐	☐
3	A	☐	☐	☐	☐	☐
4	K	☐	☐	☐	☐	☐
5	C	☐	☐	☐	☐	☐
6	G	☐	☐	☐	☐	☐
7	E	☐	☐	☐	☐	☐
8	H	☐	☐	☐	☐	☐
9	A	☐	☐	☐	☐	☐
10	G	☐	☐	☐	☐	☐
Total		**/10**				

What do you think is going well so far?

What do you need to do in order to improve?

Review the problems:

Before you give up, think of the reasons you held on
so long
— Drake

Home Work 2.1.2 — So I don't forget

Directions: Time yourself while answering these questions. Try your best to complete them in ten minutes or less! When you are done, write how long the ten problems actually took you to complete. Check your answers with the key you received, and grade yourself.

1. What is the slope of the line that passes through the points $(-6, -7)$ and $(0, -3)$?

   A. $-\dfrac{3}{2}$

   B. $-\dfrac{2}{3}$

   C. $\dfrac{2}{3}$

   D. $\dfrac{3}{2}$

   E. $\dfrac{5}{3}$

2. What is the slope of a line parallel to the graph of the equation $y = -x - 8$ in the standard (x, y) coordinate plane?

   F. -9

   G. -8

   H. -1

   J. 1

   K. 8

3. If a line with the equation $y = 2x - 3$ is perpendicular to a line with the equation $y = kx + 4$, what is the value of k?

   A. -3

   B. -2

   C. $-\dfrac{1}{2}$

   D. $\dfrac{1}{2}$

   E. 2

4. What values of x are solutions to $x^2 + x - 12$?

   F. 4 and 3

   G. 4 and -3

   H. -4 and 3

   J. -4 and -3

   K. 12 and -1

5. If a parabola crosses the x-axis at -1 and 3, which of the following is a possible equation of the parabola?

   A. $x^2 + 2$

   B. $x^2 - 2x - 3$

   C. $x^2 - 2x + 3$

   D. $x^2 + 2x - 3$

   E. $x^2 + 2x + 3$

242

6. What is the equation of a line parallel to the line with the equation $y = 2x - 5$ that passes through the point $(0, 1)$?

    F. $y = 2x - 2$

    G. $y = 2x + 1$

    H. $y = \frac{x}{2} + 1$

    J. $y = -\frac{x}{2} - 2$

    K. $y = -\frac{x}{2} + 1$

7. How many real solutions does the quadratic equation $x^2 + 1 = 0$ have?

    A. 0
    B. 1
    C. 2
    D. 3
    E. 4

8. If the line with the equation $y = ax + d$ has a greater slope than the line with the equation $y = bx + d$, what must be true about the relationship between a and b?

    F. $a = b$

    G. $a > b$

    H. $a < b$

    J. $a = 0$

    K. $b = 0$

9. What is the slope of the line that passes through the points $(3, -1)$ and $(4, -4)$?

    A. -5

    B. -3

    C. $-\frac{1}{3}$

    D. $\frac{1}{3}$

    E. 3

10. Which of the following is the graph of the linear equation $= 2x$?

F.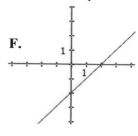

G.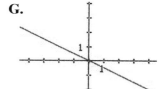

H.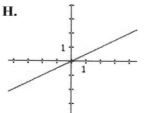

J.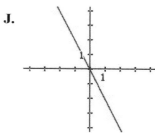

K.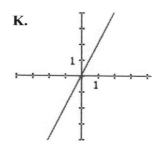

Question	Answer	Correct?	Lucky Guess	Knew It	Simple Mistake	Need Practice
1	C	☐	☐	☐	☐	☐
2	H	☐	☐	☐	☐	☐
3	C	☐	☐	☐	☐	☐
4	H	☐	☐	☐	☐	☐
5	B	☐	☐	☐	☐	☐
6	G	☐	☐	☐	☐	☐
7	A	☐	☐	☐	☐	☐
8	G	☐	☐	☐	☐	☐
9	B	☐	☐	☐	☐	☐
10	K	☐	☐	☐	☐	☐
Total		/10				

SELF-ASSESSMENT ZONE

What do you think is going well so far?

What do you need to do in order to improve?

Review the problems:

You must do the thing you think you cannot do.
— Eleanor Roosevelt

Home Work 2.2.1 — Day After

Directions: Time yourself while answering these questions. Try your best to complete them in ten minutes or less! When you are done, write how long the ten problems actually took you to complete. Check your answers with the key you received, and grade yourself.

1. In the standard (x, y) coordinate plane, the midpoint of QS is (-4, 2). If point Q is located at (-5,0) and point S is located at (x, y), what is the value of $x - y$?

   A. 1
   B. -1
   C. -3
   D. -5.5
   E. -7

2. The sides of a square are 6 cm long. One vertex of the square is at (6, -6). On a square coordinate grid marked in centimeter units, which of the following points could also be a vertex of the square?

   F. (6, 6)
   G. (12, -6)
   H. (0, 6)
   J. (-6, 0)
   K. (12, 6)

3. In the standard (x, y) coordinate plane, point P is at (0, 4) and point R is at (0, -3). What is PR?

   A. 7
   B. $5\sqrt{2}$
   C. 8
   D. $6\sqrt{2}$
   E. 10

4. If point T has a nonzero x coordinate and a nonzero y coordinate, and the x and y coordinates have the same sign, in which of 4 quadrants *must* point T be located?

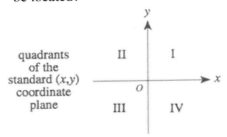

   F. I only
   G. II only
   H. III only
   J. I or II only
   K. I or III only

246

5. The circle shown below has center (-2, 5) and is tangent to the y-axis at (0, 5). What is the equation of the circle?

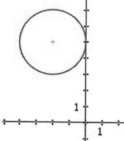

A. $(x - 2)^2 + (y + 5)^2 = 2$

B. $(x + 2)^2 + (y - 5)^2 = 2$

C. $(x - 2)^2 + (y + 5)^2 = 4$

D. $(x + 2)^2 + (y - 5)^2 = 4$

E. $(x - 5)^2 + (y + 2)^2 = 4$

6. The coordinate graph is measured in centimeter units. What is the area of the triangle shown below, in square centimeters?

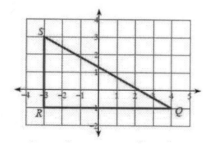

F. 40

G. 32

H. 28

J. 16

K. 14

7. Three vertices of a square are shown below. Which of the following are the coordinates of the fourth vertex?

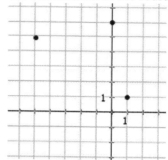

A. (0, -4)

B. (0, 4)

C. (-4, 0)

D. (4, -1)

E. (4, 0)

8. What is the distance between the coordinates (-4, -3) and (-1, 3)?

F. 3

G. 4

H. 6

J. $2\sqrt{10}$

K. $3\sqrt{5}$

9. In the standard (x, y) coordinate plane, if a segment has one endpoint at (-2, 6) and a midpoint at (1, 7), what are the coordinates of the other endpoint?

A. (-3, -1)

B. (-1, -1)

C. (-.5, 6.5)

D. (2, 6)

E. (4, 8)

10. AB is a diameter of a circle with center O. If point A is located at (-5, 3) and point B is located at (0, 4), what is the coordinate of point O?

   F. (-2.5, .5)

   G. (-2.5, 3.5)

   H. (2.5, -.5)

   J. (2.5, .5)

   K. (0, 3.5)

If you're not making mistakes, then you're not doing anything. I'm positive that a doer makes mistakes.
– John Wooden

SELF-ASSESSMENT ZONE

Question	Answer	Correct?	Lucky Guess	Knew It	Simple Mistake	Need Practice
1	E	☐	☐	☐	☐	☐
2	G	☐	☐	☐	☐	☐
3	A	☐	☐	☐	☐	☐
4	K	☐	☐	☐	☐	☐
5	D	☐	☐	☐	☐	☐
6	K	☐	☐	☐	☐	☐
7	C	☐	☐	☐	☐	☐
8	K	☐	☐	☐	☐	☐
9	E	☐	☐	☐	☐	☐
10	G	☐	☐	☐	☐	☐
Total		/10				

What do you think is going well so far?

What do you need to do in order to improve?

Review the problems:

i

Even if you fall on your face, you're still moving
forward.
— Victor Kiam

Home Work 2.2.2 — So I don't forget

Directions: Time yourself while answering these questions. Try your best to complete them in ten minutes or less! When you are done, write how long the ten problems actually took you to complete. Check your answers with the key you received, and grade yourself.

1. What is the midpoint of the segment with endpoints (-3, 8) and (-5, -1)?

    A. (1, 4.5)

    B. (1, 3.5)

    C. (-4, 3.5)

    D. (4, 4.5)

    E. (-1, -3.5)

2. A circle with center (-5, 0) is tangent to the y-axis at the origin. What is the equation of this circle, as shown below?

    F. $x^2 + (y + 5)^2 = 5$

    G. $x^2 + (y + 5)^2 = 25$

    H. $(x + 5)^2 + y^2 = 5$

    J. $(x + 5)^2 + y^2 = 25$

    K. $(x - 5)^2 + y^2 = 25$

3. A circle with center P has diameter RS. Point R has coordinates (1, 8), and point S has coordinates (-1, -4). What is PS?

    A. 37

    B. 30

    C. $2\sqrt{37}$

    D. $4\sqrt{37}$

    E. $\sqrt{37}$

4. Three vertices of a rectangle are shown below, in the standard (x, y) coordinate plane. Which of the following could be the coordinates of the fourth vertex?

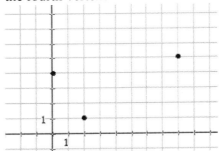

    F. (6, 8)

    G. (8, 6)

    H. (2, 7)

    J. (6, 7)

    K. (7, 8)

5. In the standard (x, y) coordinate plane, a circle has the equation $(x + 1)^2 + (y - 1)^2 = 34$. What is the radius and center of the circle?

	radius	center
A.	34	(-1, 1)
B.	$\sqrt{34}$	(-1, 1)
C.	34	(1, -1)
D.	17	(1, -1)
E.	$\sqrt{34}$	(1, -1)

6. In the standard (x, y) coordinate plane, segment AB has its midpoint at (-1, 6). If point A is located at (0, 5), what are the coordinates of point B?

    F. (-2, 7)

    G. (-1, 1)

    H. (-1, 11)

    J. (-.5, 5.5)

    K. (.5, 5.5)

7. In the standard (x, y) coordinate plane, what is the distance between the points (1, 5) and (13, 0)?

    A. 12

    B. 13

    C. $2\sqrt{30}$

    D. 15

    E. $4\sqrt{15}$

8. The line $x + y = 3$ passes through which of the 4 quadrants, as shown below?

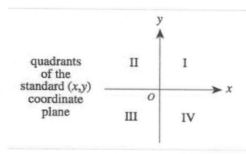

    F. I only

    G. I and II only

    H. I and IV only

    J. I, II, and III only

    K. I, II, and IV only

9. Triangles ABC and DEF are graphed below in the standard (x, y) coordinate plane. What is the difference in their areas, in square units?

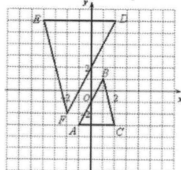

    A. 4

    B. 6

    C. 18

    D. 24

    E. 30

10. The sides of a square are 3 cm long. One vertex of the square is at (-3, -3). On a square coordinate grid marked in centimeter units, which of the following points could also be a vertex of the square?

    F. (-3, 3)

    G. (3, -3)

    H. (0, 3)

    J. (3, 0)

    K. (0, 0)

Question	Answer	Correct?	Lucky Guess	Knew It	Simple Mistake	Need Practice
		SELF-ASSESSMENT ZONE				
1	C	☐	☐	☐	☐	☐
2	J	☐	☐	☐	☐	☐
3	B	☐	☐	☐	☐	☐
4	F	☐	☐	☐	☐	☐
5	B	☐	☐	☐	☐	☐
6	F	☐	☐	☐	☐	☐
7	B	☐	☐	☐	☐	☐
8	K	☐	☐	☐	☐	☐
9	C	☐	☐	☐	☐	☐
10	K	☐	☐	☐	☐	☐
Total		/10				

What do you think is going well so far?

What do you need to do in order to improve?

Review the problems:

Don't let the fear of striking out hold you back.
—Babe Ruth

Homework 3.1.1 — Day After

Directions: Time yourself while answering these questions. Try your best to complete them in ten minutes or less! When you are done, write how long the ten problems actually took you to complete. Check your answers with the key you received, and grade yourself.

1. What is the area in square feet of triangle ABC?

A. 72

B. 84

C. 87.5

D. 168

E. 175

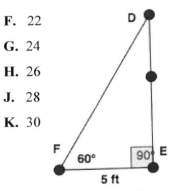

2. Triangle DEF is a 30-60-90 triangle. The length of segment FE is 5 feet. What is the perimeter to the nearest foot of triangle DEF?

F. 22

G. 24

H. 26

J. 28

K. 30

3. In the octagon below, adjacent sides meet at right angles, segment AH is 9 feet long, segment GF is 18 feet long and segment FE is 25 feet long. What is the perimeter of the figure in feet?

A. 52

B. 104

C. 156

D. 208

E. 260

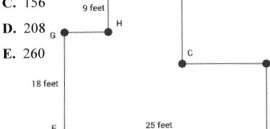

4. In the figure below, F, E, D, and A are collinear. If angle FEB = 120°, angle EBD = 41° and angle BAD = 59°, what is the degree measure of angle ABD?

F. 12°

G. 16°

H. 20°

J. 24°

K. 28°

5. Segments AC and BD are diameters of circle O and 16 inches long. What is the area of triangle AOE in square inches?

A. 16

B. 32

C. 32√2

D. 64

E. 64√2

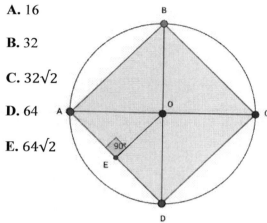
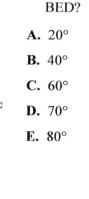

7. The figure below is a regular hexagon (6 congruent sides and angles). Two sides of the hexagon are extended to intersect at an external point E. What is the measure of angle BED?

A. 20°

B. 40°

C. 60°

D. 70°

E. 80°

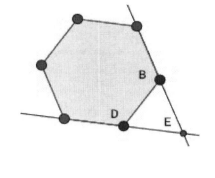

6. The bases of the isosceles trapezoid shown below are 18 centimeters and 28 centimeters.
What is the distance, in centimeters, between these two parallel sides?

F. 8

G. 9

H. 10

J. 12

K. 13

257

Question	Answer	Correct?	Lucky Guess	Knew It	Simple Mistake	Need Practice
		SELF-ASSESSMENT ZONE				
1	B	☐	☐	☐	☐	☐
2	G	☐	☐	☐	☐	☐
3	B	☐	☐	☐	☐	☐
4	H	☐	☐	☐	☐	☐
5	A	☐	☐	☐	☐	☐
6	J	☐	☐	☐	☐	☐
7	C	☐	☐	☐	☐	☐
Total		/7				

What do you think is going well so far?

What do you need to do in order to improve?

Review the problems:

Education is what allows you to stand out

— Ellen Ochoa

Home Work 3.1.2 — So I don't forget

Directions: Time yourself while answering these questions. Try your best to complete them in ten minutes or less! When you are done, write how long the ten problems actually took you to complete. Check your answers with the key you received, and grade yourself.

For problems 1 and 2 use the figure below.
Angle FAD = 90°, angle FDE = 45° and
segment FA is 10 inches long.

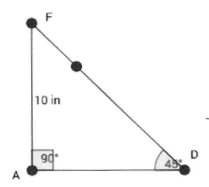

1. What is the area, to the nearest square inch, of triangle FAD?
   - **A.** 50
   - **B.** 71
   - **C.** 87
   - **D.** 141
   - **E.** 173

2. What is the perimeter, to the nearest inch of triangle FAD?
   - **F.** 24
   - **G.** 30
   - **H.** 34
   - **J.** 35
   - **K.** 37

For problems 3 and 4 use the figure below.

Line AB is parallel to line EC, and line AE is parallel to line BC. Line BD is perpendicular to line EC, segment ED is 11 feet long, segment BC is 10 feet long, and segment BD is 8 feet long. Angle AEC is approx. 127°.

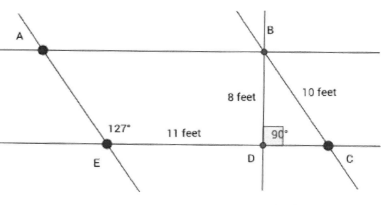

3. To the nearest square foot, what is the area of parallelogram ABCE?
   - **A.** 80
   - **B.** 88
   - **C.** 110
   - **D.** 136
   - **E.** 1016

260

4. To the nearest degree, what is the measure of angle CBD?

F. 33°

G. 37°

H. 53°

J. 77°

K. 127°

5. The figure below is a regular pentagon. What is the sum of angles 1, 2, 3, 4 and 5?

A. 180

B. 270

C. 360

D. 540

E. 720

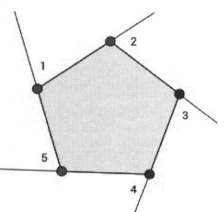

7. The area of a rectangle is 119 square inches. The rectangle's length is 3 feet less than twice its width. What is the perimeter, in inches, of the rectangle?

A. 27

B. 39.7

C. 45

D. 58

E. 67

6. The legs of a right triangle have lengths 3 feet and 4 feet respectively. The legs of a similar right triangle have lengths 12 feet and 16 feet respectively. What is the length, in feet of hypotenuse of the larger triangle?

F. 5

G. 10

H. 15

J. 20

K. not enough information given

261

Question	Answer	Correct?	Lucky Guess	Knew It	Simple Mistake	Need Practice
1	A	☐	☐	☐	☐	☐
2	H	☐	☐	☐	☐	☐
3	D	☐	☐	☐	☐	☐
4	G	☐	☐	☐	☐	☐
5	C	☐	☐	☐	☐	☐
6	J	☐	☐	☐	☐	☐
7	C	☐	☐	☐	☐	☐
Total		/7				

SELF-ASSESSMENT ZONE

What do you think is going well so far?

What do you need to do in order to improve?

Review the problems:

Follow your passion. Stay true to yourself. Never follow someone else's path unless you're in the woods and you're lost and you see a path. By all means, you should follow that.

— Ellen DeGeneres

Home Work 3.2.1 — Day After

Directions: Time yourself while answering these questions. Try your best to complete them in ten minutes or less! When you are done, write how long the ten problems actually took you to complete. Check your answers with the key you received, and grade yourself.

1. What is $sinA$?

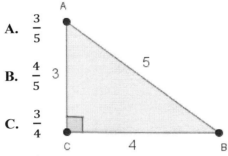

A. $\frac{3}{5}$

B. $\frac{4}{5}$

C. $\frac{3}{4}$

D. $\frac{4}{3}$

E. $\frac{5}{3}$

2. The graph of $f(x) = cosx$ is shown. How will the graph of $f(-x)$ change from the graph of $f(x)$?

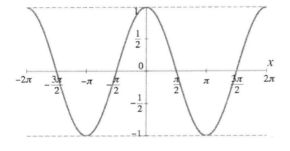

F. reflected about the $x - axis$
G. shifted one unit up
H. shifted one unit down
J. shifted one unit right
K. no change

3. Anne, who is standing at point A, is trying to determine which friend she should swim to in order to swim the shorter length. Ben is standing at point B, and Cassidy is at point C. Anne knows Ben and Cassidy are 12 m apart and the following angle measures: $m < ACB = 102°$ and $m < ABC = 68°$. To whom should she swim and how can she determine which length is shorter?

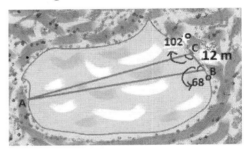

A. Ben; The Law of Cosines

B. Ben; in a triangle, the side opposite the largest angle is longest

C. Cassidy; The Law of Cosines

D. Cassidy; in a triangle, the side opposite the largest angle is longest

E. cannot be determined from the information given

4. If 4 of 10 shirts are dressy, what is the probability that you will randomly choose a shirt that is not dressy?

    F. 0.4

    G. 0.6

    H. 0.8

    J. 1.4

    K. 1.6

5. $\cos^2 B = ?$

    A. $\dfrac{\sqrt{7}}{3}$

    B. $\dfrac{2\sqrt{7}}{3}$

    C. $\dfrac{7}{9}$

    D. $\dfrac{\sqrt{2}}{3}$

    E. $\dfrac{2}{9}$

6. Which of the following is an expression for the length of side AB? (The Law of Sines states that $\dfrac{sinA}{a} = \dfrac{sinB}{b} = \dfrac{sinC}{c}$ for any triangle ABC, where a is the side opposite angle A, b is the side opposite angle B, and c is the side opposite angle C)

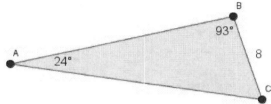

    F. $\dfrac{8sin63°}{sin24°}$

    G. $\dfrac{8sin24°}{sin63°}$

    H. $\dfrac{8sin93°}{sin24°}$

    J. $\dfrac{sin63°}{8sin24°}$

    K. $\dfrac{sin93°}{8sin63°}$

7. The prom planning committee consists of 1 junior and 2 seniors. If there are 225 juniors and 240 seniors, how many different combinations are there for the prom planning committee?

    A. 465

    B. 54,000

    C. 108,000

    D. 12,906,000

    E. 12,960,000

Question	Answer	Correct?	Lucky Guess	Knew It	Simple Mistake	Need Practice
1	B	☐	☐	☐	☐	☐
2	K	☐	☐	☐	☐	☐
3	D	☐	☐	☐	☐	☐
4	G	☐	☐	☐	☐	☐
5	C	☐	☐	☐	☐	☐
6	F	☐	☐	☐	☐	☐
7	D	☐	☐	☐	☐	☐
Total		/7				

SELF-ASSESSMENT ZONE

What do you think is going well so far?

What do you need to do in order to improve?

Review the problems:

I hear and I forget. I see and I remember. I do
and I understand.
— Chinese Proverb

Home Work 3.2.2 — So I don't forget

Directions: Time yourself while answering these questions. Try your best to complete them in ten minutes or less! When you are done, write how long the ten problems actually took you to complete. Check your answers with the key you received, and grade yourself.

For problems 1 and 2, use the figure below.

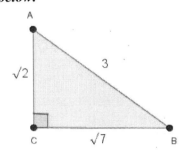

1. $sin^2 A + cos^2 B = ?$

   A. $\dfrac{2\sqrt{7}}{3}$

   B. $\dfrac{49}{9}$

   C. $\dfrac{14}{18}$

   D. $\dfrac{7}{9}$

   E. $\dfrac{14}{9}$

2. What is $tanB$?

   F. $\dfrac{\sqrt{2}}{3}$

   G. $\dfrac{\sqrt{7}}{3}$

   H. $\dfrac{\sqrt{14}}{2}$

   J. $\dfrac{\sqrt{2}}{\sqrt{7}}$

   K. $\dfrac{2}{7}$

3. A bag contains 20 yellow marbles, 15 blue marbles, and 15 red marbles. If you randomly pick one marble from the bag, what is the probability that the marble you pick is NOT blue?

   A. 0.3

   B. 0.43

   C. 0.7

   D. 0.85

   E. 1.3

4. Which of the following is the correct expression for the length of side AB?

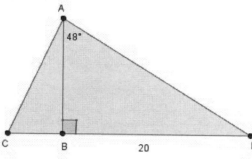

F. $\dfrac{20sin42}{sin48}$

G. $\dfrac{20sin48}{sin42}$

H. $\dfrac{sin42}{20sin48}$

J. $20sin42sin48$

K. $\dfrac{20}{sin42sin48}$

5. Your classmate wants to find the length of side AC. Which of the following will allow him to find it?

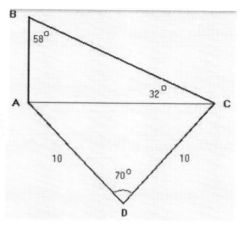

A. Law of Sines:

$$\frac{sinA}{a} = \frac{sinB}{b} = \frac{sinC}{c}$$

B. Law of Cosines:
$$c^2 = a^2 + b^2 - 2abcos(c)$$

C. Pythagorean Theorem:
$$a^2 + b^2 = c^2$$

D. The side opposite the largest angle is the longest side

E. *not enough information*

6. You are drawing two cards from a standard deck, without replacing the first card. What is the expression for the probability of drawing two kings? (*note: there are 4 kings and 52 cards total in a standard deck*)

F. $\dfrac{4}{52} \cdot \dfrac{4}{51}$

G. $\dfrac{4}{52} \cdot \dfrac{4}{52}$

H. $\dfrac{4}{52} \cdot \dfrac{3}{51}$

J. $\dfrac{4}{52} + \dfrac{3}{52}$

K. $\dfrac{4}{52} + \dfrac{3}{51}$

7. In right triangle ABC, $sinA = \dfrac{3}{5}$. What is $cosA$?

A. $\dfrac{3}{5}$

B. $\dfrac{4}{5}$

C. $\dfrac{4}{3}$

D. $\dfrac{3}{4}$

E. 1

I've missed 3000 shots. Twenty-six times the game-winning shot has been trusted to me, and I've missed. I've lost over 300 games. I've failed over and over and over again, and that is why I've succeeded.

— Michael Jordan

SELF-ASSESSMENT ZONE

Question	Answer	Correct?	Lucky Guess	Knew It	Simple Mistake	Need Practice
1	E	☐	☐	☐	☐	☐
2	J	☐	☐	☐	☐	☐
3	C	☐	☐	☐	☐	☐
4	F	☐	☐	☐	☐	☐
5	B	☐	☐	☐	☐	☐
6	H	☐	☐	☐	☐	☐
7	B	☐	☐	☐	☐	☐
Total		/7				

What do you think is going well so far?

What do you need to do in order to improve?

Review the problems:

You can be the lead in your own life

— Kerry Washington

This page intentionally left blank

Pre-Test

PRACTICE TEST 1: PRE-TEST

Directions: solve each problem and circle the correct answer

Do not spend too much time on any question. Solve what you can and return to unanswered questions in any remaining time at the end.

You are allowed to use a calculator on the test

1. The adventure club is planning an overnight camping trip to Punderson State Park. The nightly fee for camping on the grounds is \$5 per person and \$8 per vehicle. Which of the following expressions gives the total overnight amount that the Adventure Club will need to pay for p persons and v vehicles?

   A. $5v + 8p$
   B. $5p + 8V$
   C. $5(v + p)$
   D. $13(v + p)$
   E. $5(v + p) + 8p$

2. If x = 7, y = 8 and z = -5, what does $(x - z)(x - y + z)$ equal?

   F. -72
   G. -48
   H. -12
   J. 12
   K. 72

$$(7 + 5) \ (7 - 8 + -5)$$

3. A copy machine makes 100 copies a minute. A second copy machine makes 50 copies per minute. The first copy machine starts 5 minutes after the second machine starts. Both machines stop making copies 10 minutes after the second machine started. What was the total amount of copies that both machines made?

   A. 250
   B. 500
   C. 750
   D. 1000
   E. 1250

4. So far in Algebra 2, Hunter has a 90% average on the first three tests, earning an 82, 91 and 97. What is the lowest score Hunter can earn on the fourth test to maintain this average?

   F. 90
   G. 89
   H. 88
   J. 87
   K. 86

277

5. Laura earns $8.50 per hour regular pay for the first 40 hours she works each week. Laura is paid 1.5 times her regular pay for each hour over 40 hours she works in a week. How much does Laura earn working 44 hours in a week?

$40 \times 8.50 = 340$

A. $330
B. $374
C. $391
D. $475
E. $561

$\begin{array}{r} 12.75 \\ \times \quad 4 \\ \hline 51 \end{array}$

$\begin{array}{r} 340 \\ + \quad 51 \\ \hline 391 \end{array}$

6. Which of the following mathematical expressions is equivalent to the verbal expression, "A number, x, squared is 15 more than the product of 2 and x?"

F. $2x = 15 + 2x$
G. $2x = 15 + 2^x$
H. $x^2 = 15x + 2^x$
J. $x^2 = 15 + x^2$
K. $x^2 = 15 + 2x$

7. For two consecutive even integers, twice the smaller integer plus half the larger integer is -39. What are the two integers?

A. -12, -14
B. -14, -16
C. -16, -18
D. -18, -20
E. -20, -22

-28

8. Fred bought tickets for the Cav's game and received a group discount. He got them for $40.00 each and spent a total of $720.00. Fred saved a total of $441.00 by buying them at the group rate. What would each ticket have cost at regular price?

$720 \div 40 = 18$
$720 + 441 = 1161$
$1161 \div 18 = 64.5$

F. $24.50
G. $29.40
H. $58.00
J. $64.50
K. $65.40

$\begin{array}{r} 2x^2 + 5y \\ \times \quad 2x^2 - 5y \\ \hline 4x^4 - 25y \end{array}$

9. The expression $(2x^2 + 5y)(2x^2 - 5y)$ is equivalent to:

A. $4x^4 - 25y^2$
B. $4x^4 - 10y^2$
C. $4x^4 + 25y^2$
D. $4x^4 + 10y^2$
E. $4x^4 - 25y$

10. A rectangle has an area of 56 square feet and a perimeter of 30 feet. What is the longest of the side lengths, in feet, of the rectangle?

F. 4
G. 6
H. 7
J. 8
K. 9

11. In $\triangle DEF$, $m < E$ is 23°, and $< F$ is a right angle. What is the measure of $< D$?

A. 57°
B. 67°
C. 90°
D. 112°
E. 157°

12. Barry packed 5 shirts, 3 pairs of shorts, and 2 hats. How many combinations of one shirt, one pair of shorts, and one hat can Barry choose from?

F. 10
G. 15
H. 30
J. 45
K. 60

13. If $8(x + 8) = -12$, then $x =$?

A. $\frac{-19}{2}$
B. $\frac{-5}{2}$
C. $\frac{-1}{2}$
D. $\frac{1}{2}$
E. $\frac{21}{4}$

$8x + 64 = -12$
-64
$\frac{8x}{8} = \frac{-76}{8}$

14. A function $g(x) = -2x^2$. What is (-3) ?

F. -36
G. -18
H. -12
J. 18
K. 36

$x(-3) = -2x^2$
$x = -2(-3)^2$

15. If $4^x = 67$, then which of the following must be true?

A. $1 < x < 2$
B. $2 < x < 3$
C. $3 < x < 4$
D. $4 < x < 5$
E. $5 < x < 6$

16. What is the least common multiple of 20, 35, and 50?

F. 50
G. 100
H. 350
J. 700
K. 35,000

17. Spectacular Soups is designing a new cylindrical soup container for there to-go orders. If the diameter of the base is 3.5 inches and the height is 5 inches, how much soup can the container hold, rounded to the nearest cubic inch? $(V = \pi r^2 h)$

A. 27
B. 56
C. 48
D. 49
E. 141

$\pi \cdot (1.75)^2 \cdot 5$
48

3.5
5
$V = 3,143.5$

18. What is the radius, in cm, of a circle with circumference 8π cm?

F. 4
G. 8
H. 8π
J. 16
K. 16π

19. $-5|-4+6| = ?$

A. -50
B. -10
C. -3
D. 10
E. 50

$-5|4$
$-5|2|$
-10

20. y varies inversely as the square root of x. If $y = 2$ as $x = 9$, what is y when = 36 ?

F. 43
G. 29
H. 6
J. 2
K. 1

21. The lengths of the sides of the right triangle shown below are in feet. What is $\cos\theta$?

A. $\dfrac{a}{b}$
B. $\dfrac{a}{c}$
C. $\dfrac{b}{c}$
D. $\dfrac{b}{a}$
E. $\dfrac{c}{b}$

280

22. A group of cells grows at a rate described by the equation $y = 1.5(6)^t$, where t represents the number of years and y represents the population. What is the population of cells after 3 days?

F. 324
G. 368
H. 418
J. 627
K. 729

23. $(3a + 4b - 2c) - (a - 5b + 6c)$ is equivalent to:

A. $3a - 9b + 4c$
B. $3a + 9b - 8c$
C. $2a - b + 4c$
D. $2a + 9b + 4c$
E. $2a + 9b - 8c$

$3a + 4b - 2c$
$1a - 5b + 6c$

$2a + 9b - 8c$

24. In a volleyball passing drill, 5 players stand evenly spaced around the perimeter of the court. The player with the ball (the passer) must pass to another player (the receiver) that is not on her immediate left or right and cannot be the player who last passed the ball. On which pass of the ball will the first passer become the receiver?

F. 3rd
G. 4th
H. 5th
J. 8th
K. 10th

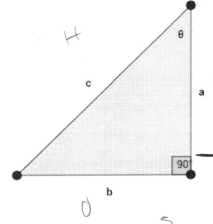

25. The lines m and n lie in an (x, y) coordinate plane. An equation for line m is $y = .75x - .25$. The slope of line n is .2 greater than the slope of line m. What is the slope of line n?

    A. -.45
    B. -.27
    C. -.23
    D. .77
    E. .95

26. The expression
$-6x^4(9x^3 - 5x^5)$ is equivalent to:

    F. $-54x^7 + 30x^9$
    G. $-54x^7 - 30x^9$
    H. $-54x^{12} + 30x^{20}$
    J. $-54x^{12} - 30x^{20}$
    K. $-24x^7$

$-54x^7 + 30x^9$

27. What is the surface area, in square inches, of a 5 inch cube?

    A. 150
    B. 125
    C. 100
    D. 60
    E. 50

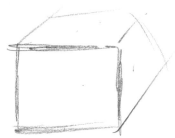

28. In right triangle ACD below, $\overline{EB} \parallel \overline{DC}$, and $\overline{EB} \perp \overline{AC}$ at B. The length of $\overline{AD}$ is 14 feet, the length of $\overline{EB}$ is 6 feet and the length of $\overline{AB}$ is 8 feet. What is the length, in feet, of $\overline{DC}$?

    F. 7
    G. 8.4
    H. 9
    J. 9.6
    K. 12

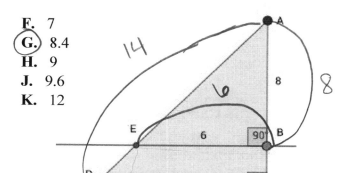

$h =$ $A = 1/2 bh$

$A =$

$y = mx + b$

$y = \dfrac{3x + 4}{1}$

281

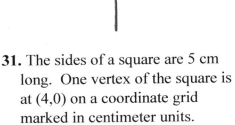

29. An automobile travels at a constant rate of speed on the Ohio Turnpike. The car starts 25 miles west of Cleveland and heads west towards Chicago. The chart below shows how far the car is from Cleveland, d miles, over 1 hour intervals from t = 0 hours to t = 5 hours.

t	0	1	2	3	4	5
d	25	100	175	250	325	400

Which of the following equations represents this data?

A. $d = t + 25$
B. $d = 25t + 75$
C. $d = 25t + 100$
D. $d = 75t + 25$
E. $d = 75t + 100$

30. The inequality $5(x - 4) < 6(x - 3)$ is equivalent to which of the following inequalities?

F. $x < -2$
G. $x > -2$
H. $x < -1$
J. $x > -1$
K. $x > 1$

31. The sides of a square are 5 cm long. One vertex of the square is at (4,0) on a coordinate grid marked in centimeter units. Which of the following coordinate pairs could be the location of another vertex of the square?

A. $(-4,0)$
B. $(0,-1)$
C. $(0,5)$
D. $(5,0)$
E. $(9,0)$

32. For $\triangle ABC$, shown below, which of the following is an expression for y in terms of x?

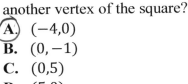

F. $x - 5$
G. $x^2 - 25$
H. $\sqrt{x^2 - 10}$
J. $\sqrt{x^2 + 25}$
K. $\sqrt{x^2 - 25}$

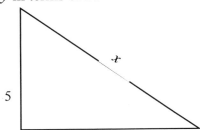

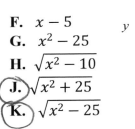

282

33. A drawer contains 12 t-shirts. Four are red, 5 are blue, and 3 are gray. How many more red shirts must be added to the drawer so that the probability of randomly picking a red shirt is $\frac{5}{9}$?

- A. 3
- B. 5
- C. 6
- D. 9
- E. 18

34. What are the quadrants of the standard (x,y) coordinate plane below that contain points on the graph of the equation $2x + y = 3$?

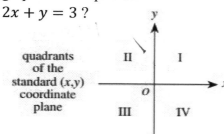

quadrants of the standard (x,y) coordinate plane

$y = -2x + 3$

- F. I and III only
- G. II and IV only
- H. I, II, and III only
- J. I, II, and IV only
- K. I, III, and IV only

35. The graph of $y = 4x^2 - 3$ passes through $(2, 4a)$ in the standard (x,y) coordinate plane. What is the value of a?

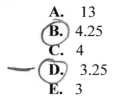

- A. 13
- B. 4.25
- C. 4
- D. 3.25
- E. 3

36. Laura, Liz, and Sarah shared a batch of cookies. Laura ate $\frac{1}{7}$ of the cookies, Liz had half of the cookies, and Sarah had the rest. What is the ratio of Laura's share to Sarah's share?

- F. 5:2
- G. 5:1
- H. 1:2
- J. 1:5
- K. 2:5

37. The equation of Circle A is $x^2 + (y - 3)^2 = 7$. What is the radius of the circle, in coordinate units, and the coordinates of the center of the circle?

	radius	center
A.	$\sqrt{7}$	$(0, -3)$
B.	7	$(0, -3)$
C.	7	$(0, 3)$
D.	$\sqrt{7}$	$(0, 3)$
E.	49	$(0, 3)$

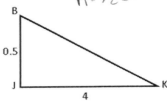

$$5y + x = 0$$
$$5x = -x$$
$$\frac{5x}{5} = \frac{-x}{5}$$
$$y = -5x$$

38. The figure below consists of a square and 2 semicircles, with dimensions as shown. What is the total area, in square centimeters, of the figure?

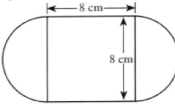

|← 8 cm →|

8 cm

F. $16 + 16\pi$
G. $16 + 64\pi$
H. $64 + 8\pi$
J. $64 + 16\pi$
K. $64 + 64\pi$

39. A circle with a radius of 3 centimeters is inscribed in a square. What is the area, in square centimeters, of the shaded region of the square?

A. $36 - 9\pi$
B. $36 - 6\pi$
C. $12 - 6\pi$
D. $9 - 9\pi$
E. $9 - 6\pi$

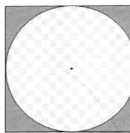

40. The coordinates of the endpoints of segment $\overline{AB}$ are $A(-3, 7)$ and $B(0, 4)$. What is the y-coordinate of the midpoint of $\overline{AB}$?

F. 11
G. 6.5
H. 5.5
J. 5
K. -1.5

41. Which of the following best describes the graph of the following system of equations in an *(x, y)* coordinate plane?

$$2y + 3x = 6$$
$$3y - 2x = -6$$

I. 2 perpendicular lines
II. 2 parallel lines
III. 2 intersecting lines
IV. A single line

A. I only
B. II only
C. III only
D. IV only
E. I and III

42. What is the area of triangle BJK in square feet?

$A = \frac{1}{2}bh$

F. 1
G. 2
H. 3
J. 4
K. 5

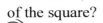

43. What is the solution for the following system of equations?
$$3x - y = 12$$
$$8x + 3y = -2$$

A. $(-2, -18)$
B. $(-1, -15)$
C. $(0, -12)$
D. $(1, -9)$
E. $(2, -6)$

44. Wild Bill rode 60 miles due west from Deadwood after a card game. According to the measurements in the chart below, which of the following expressions gives the distance, in miles, between Wild Bill and Devils Tower?

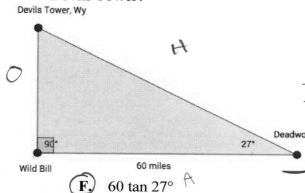

Devils Tower, Wy

O

90°   27°

Wild Bill   60 miles

Deadwood S.D.

F. 60 tan 27°   A

G. 60 cos 27°

H. 60 sin 27°

J. $\dfrac{60}{\cos 27°}$

K. $\dfrac{60}{\sin 27°}$

tan 27=

45. In the figure, $\overleftrightarrow{EA} \parallel \overleftrightarrow{DB}$, and $\overrightarrow{DC}$ bisects $\angle EDB$. If $m\angle EDB = 60°$ and DE = 10 inches, what is the area of triangle DEB in square inches?

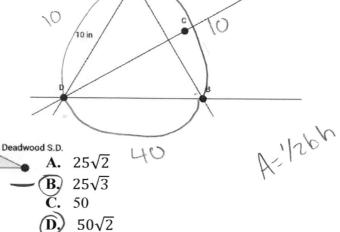

10 in

10   10

40

A. $25\sqrt{2}$

B. $25\sqrt{3}$

C. 50

D. $50\sqrt{2}$

E. $50\sqrt{3}$

A=1/2bh

Use the following information
to answer questions 46 – 48.

In the figure below, ABCDEFGH
and polygon IJKLMNOP are
regular octagons. All segments
intersect at the indicated points.
JK = 2 feet.

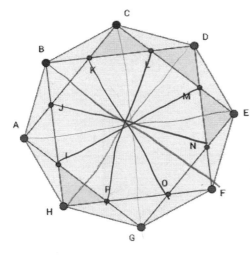

47. If octagon ABCDEFGH were
inscribed in a circle, what would
be the length of its diameter $\overline{AE}$ in
feet?

    A. $2 + 2\sqrt{2}$
    B. 6
    C. $4 + 2\sqrt{2}$
    D. 8
    E. 9

48. What is the area, in square feet,
of regular octagon IJKLMNOP?

    F. $1 + \sqrt{2}$
    G. $8 + 8\sqrt{2}$
    H. $2 + 2\sqrt{2}$
    J. $4 + 4\sqrt{2}$
    K. 16

46. The design of the figure above
has now many lines of symmetry?

    F. 2
    G. 4
    H. 8
    J. 16
    K. 32

Use the following information to answer questions 49 – 50.

In the circle shown below, O is the center with a radius of 8 cm.
$\overrightarrow{MP}$ bisects $\angle AMB$.
$\angle ABM$
$= 45°$ & $\overleftrightarrow{AB}$ and $\overleftrightarrow{OM}$ intersect at B.
$\overleftrightarrow{AM}$ and $\overleftrightarrow{OM}$ intersect at M.

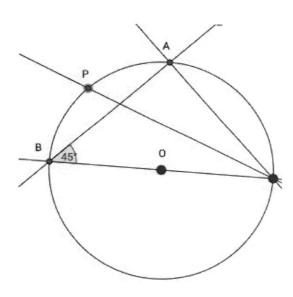

49. What is the length of chord AB in centimeters?

A. 6
B. 8
C. 10
D. $8\sqrt{2}$
E. $8\sqrt{3}$

50. What is the measure of arc AP?

F. 11.25°
G. 22.5°
H. 30°
J. 45°
K. 60°

51. The determinant of a matrix $\begin{bmatrix} a & b \\ c & d \end{bmatrix}$ equals $ad - bc$. What must be the value of x in order for the matrix $\begin{bmatrix} x & -6 \\ -1 & x \end{bmatrix}$ to have a determinant of 10?

A. -16
B. -4
C. -2
D. 2
E. 16

52. The amount of bacteria in the colony after x hours is given by the equation
$y = 2(1 + r)^x$, where r is the growth rate. If there were 28 bacteria after 3 hours, what is the growth rate of the bacteria in the colony? Round to the nearest tenth.

F. 0.5
G. 1.4
H. 1.5
J. 2.1
K. 2.4

$y = 2(1 + 28)^3$

$2 + 2r^3$

$2 + 56$

58^3

53. Cylinder A has a surface area of 20 square units. What is Cylinder A's height, expressed solely in terms of r?

(*Surface Area of a cylinder* $= 2\pi r^2 + 2\pi rh$)

   A. $10 - r$

   B. $r(10\pi - 1)$

   C. $r(10\pi r - 1)$

   D. $\frac{10}{\pi r} - r$

   E. $2\pi r^2 + 40\pi r$

54. If $x < -1$ and $0 < y < 1$, which of the following must be true?

   F. $-1 < xy < 0$

   G. $0 < xy < 1$

   H. $xy < -1$

   J. $-1 < \frac{x}{y} < 0$

   K. $\frac{x}{y} < -1$

55. $\triangle ABC$ and $\triangle PQR$ are shown below. If $PR = 42$ cm, what is a possible length of $\overline{AC}$?

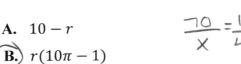

$\frac{70}{x} = \frac{110}{42}$

   A.   40 cm

   B.   42 cm

   C.   44 cm

   D.   46 cm

   E.   50 cm

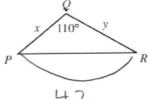

42

$\frac{70}{110} = \frac{x}{42}$

$\frac{110x}{110} = \frac{2940}{110}$

$x =$

56. Which of the following equations represents a graph 4 units left and 3 units down from its parent function, $y = x^2$?

   F. $y = (x - 4)^2 - 3$

   G. $y = (x + 4)^2 - 3$

   H. $y = (x - 3)^2 - 4$

   J. $y = (x + 3)^2 - 4$

   K. $y = (x + 4)^2 + 3$

57. What is the sum of the first 4 terms of the arithmetic sequence in which the 7th term is -2 and the 12th term is -17?

   A.   56

   B.   49

   C.   46

   D.   39

   E.   -19

58. Which of the following represents the solution set of the following inequality?

$$|x + 5| < -3$$

F. $(-\infty, -8)$

G. $(-8, -2)$

H. $(-\infty, -8) \cup (-2, \infty)$

J. $(-\infty, -2) \cup (-8, \infty)$

K. The empty set

59. An angle θ is located in the third quadrant of the standard (x, y) coordinate plane. If $\sec\theta = -\frac{26}{10}$, what is $\cot\theta$?

A. $-\frac{26}{10}$

B. $-\frac{24}{10}$

C. $-\frac{10}{24}$

D. $\frac{10}{24}$

E. $\frac{26}{10}$

60. What is the real value of x in the equation

$$\log_2 24 - \log_2 3 = \log_5 x?$$

F. 3

G. 21

H. 72

J. 125

K. 243

Do not go on until you are out of time

STOP

289

PRACTICE TEST 1: PRE-TEST KEY

1.	B	42.	F
2.	F	43.	E
3.	D	44.	F
4.	F	45.	B
5.	C	46.	H
6.	K	47.	C
7.	B	48.	G
8.	J	49.	D
9.	A	50.	J
10.	J	51.	B
11.	B	52.	G
12.	H	53.	D
13.	A	54.	K
14.	G	55.	A
15.	C	56.	G
16.	J	57.	A
17.	C	58.	K
18.	F	59.	D
19.	B	60.	J
20.	K		
21.	B		
22.	F		
23.	E		
24.	H		
25.	E		
26.	F		
27.	A		
28.	G		
29.	D		
30.	G		
31.	E		
32.	K		
33.	C		
34.	J		
35.	D		
36.	K		
37.	D		
38.	J		
39.	A		
40.	H		
41.	E		

Scoring Guide

ACT® Score	Raw Score
36	59 – 60
35	57 – 58
34	55 – 56
33	54
32	53
31	52
30	50 – 51
29	49
28	47 – 48
27	45 – 46
26	43 – 44
25	41 – 42
24	38 – 40
23	36 – 37
22	34 – 35
21	33
20	31 – 32
19	29 – 30
18	27 – 28
17	24 – 26
16	19 – 23
15	15 – 18
14	12 – 14
13	10 - 11
12	8 – 9
11	6 – 7
10	5
9	4
8	–
7	3
6	–
5	2
4	–
3	1
2	–
1	0

SELF-ASSESSMENT ZONE

Raw Score		ACT® Score	

How was your time management?

Asses yourself	I did ok	I was a little challenged	I was very challenged
Long word problems	☐	☐	☐
Trigonometry problems	☐	☐	☐
Basic Algebra Problems	☐	☐	☐
Geometry Problems	☐	☐	☐
Fraction Problems	☐	☐	☐
Parentage Problems	☐	☐	☐

What do you think is going well so far?

What do you need to do in order to improve?

Post-Test

PRACTICE TEST 2: POST-TEST

Directions: solve each problem and circle the correct answer

Do not spend too much time on any question. Solve what you can and return to unanswered questions in any remaining time at the end.

You are allowed to use a calculator on the test

PRACTICE TEST 2: POST-TEST

60 Minutes—60 Questions

1. The Weekly fee for staying at Sunny Beach Camp is $15 per vehicle and $7 per person. What equation can you use to calculate how much it would cost to stay with p people and v vehicles for one week?

   A. $15v + 7p$

   B. $22(v + p)$

   C. $15p + 7v$

   D. $15(v + p)$

   E. $7(v + p)$

2. If $g = 12$, $z = -3$, and $q = 2$. What does $(g - z + q)(z + q)$ equal?

   F. 16

   G. 17

   H. -11

   J. -17

   K. 11

3. A copy machine makes 45 copies per minute. A second copy machine makes 120 copies per minute. The first machine starts making copies 3 minutes after the second one starts. They both stop 10 minutes after the second one starts. How many copies are made?

   A. 1650

   B. 1290

   C. 1200

   D. 810

   E. 1515

4. Jordan has rolled a die 6 times getting 2, 5, 3, 6, and 4. What must Jordan roll to get maintain the exact average?

   F. 1

   G. 2

   H. 3

   J. 4

   K. 5

5. Sarah earns $9.20 an hour for her regular 40 hours. Any time over she is paid 1.5 times her regular pay. How much would Sarah earn if she works 43 hours?

   A. $395.60

   B. $579.60

   C. $409.40

   D. $368.00

   E. $47.50

295

6. Which of the following equations is equivalent to the verbal expression "A number, x, squared is 42 less than the product of 6 and x.

   F. $2x = 6x - 42$
   G. $x^2 = 6x - 42$
   H. $2x = 42 - 6x$
   J. $x^2 = 42 - 6x$
   K. $x^2 = 42 - x^6$

7. If $5(x - 5) = -9$ then $x = ?$

   A. $\frac{16}{5}$

   B. $\frac{-16}{5}$

   C. $\frac{-39}{5}$

   D. $\frac{-3}{5}$

   E. $\frac{3}{5}$

8. A soccer tournament offers discount tickets for $8. Juan bought $288 on tickets and saved $108. How much are regular tickets?

   F. $11.00
   G. $10.50
   H. $3.00
   J. $12.00
   K. $10.00

9. The expression $(4x - 2y^2)(4x + 2y^2)$ Is equivalent to?

   A. $(16x^2 - 8y^4)$
   B. $(16x^2 + 4y^4)$
   C. $(8x^2 - 8y^4)$
   D. $(16x^2 - 4y^4)$
   E. $(8x^2 - 4y^4)$

10. A rectangle has an area of 24 inches and a perimeter of 20 inches. What is the length of the shortest side in inches?

    F. 5
    G. 6
    H. 4
    J. 3
    K. 7

11. In $\triangle XYZ$, $m < X$ is 65° and $< Y$ is a right angle. What is the measure of $< Z$?

    A. 250°
    B. 205°
    C. 155°
    D. 70°
    E. 25°

12. Jared has packed 6 shirts, 4 pants, 3 hats and 2 pairs of shoes. How many outfits can Jared choose from?

F. 15
G. 25
H. 50
J. 144
K. 155

13. For two consecutive integers, three times the smaller and half the larger is 74

A. 20, 21
B. 21, 22
C. 23, 24
D. 20, 28
E. 22, 16

14. A function of $g(x) = 6x^2$. What is $g(-5)$?

F. -150
G. -30
H. 30
J. 25
K. 150

15. If $4^x = 560$, then which of the following must be true?

A. $1 < x < 2$
B. $2 < x < 3$
C. $3 < x < 4$
D. $4 < x < 5$
E. $5 < x$

16. What is the least common multiple of 30, 20, and 45?

F. 20
G. 90
H. 180
J. 300
K. 360

17. Fantastic Phones is designing the packaging for their new phone. The box is a Triangular prism with a height of 12 inches, a base of 6 inches, and a volume of 468 cubic inches. What is the length, in inches, of the prism? ($V = \frac{1}{2} * b * h * l$)

A. 13
B. 19.5
C. 26
D. 3.25
E. 6.5

18. Four points R, S, T, and U lie on a circle that is 22 units in circumference. R is 10 units counter clockwise from S. T is 13 units clockwise from S. U is 4 units clockwise from S. What is the order clockwise from S?

F. S, U, T, R
G. S, T, R, U
H. S, T, U, R
J. S, R, U, T
K. S, U, R, T

19. A group of cells grow at a rate described by the equation $y = 15(9)^t$, Where t represents the number of days and y represents the population. What is the population of the cells after 2.5 days?

A. 243
B. 3645
C. 337.5
D. 211755.36
E. 7845.79

20. The width of a rectangle is 4 times the width of a smaller rectangle. They have the same length. The area of the smaller rectangle is A. The area of the larger triangle is kA. What is k?

F. 1/2
G. 2
H. 3/5
J. 4
K. 1/4

21. Lines a and b lie in the standard (x, y) coordinate plane. The equation for the line a is $y = 6.75x + 450$. The slope of the line b is 0.65 greater than the slope of the line a what is the slope of the line b?

A. 4.39
B. 6.1
C. 450.65
D. 292.50
E. 7.4

22. $(7x - 5y + 2z) - (2x + 3y - 2z)$ is equivalent to:

F. $5x - 8y + 4z$
G. $5x - 2y$
H. $9x - 2y$
J. $9x - 8y + 4z$
K. $5x - 2y + 4z$

23. The right triangle below is labeled. What is sin θ

A. $\frac{A}{B}$
B. $\frac{A}{C}$
C. $\frac{B}{C}$
D. $\frac{B}{A}$
E. $\frac{C}{B}$

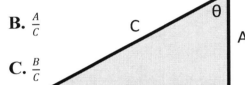

24. At baseball practice 5 players are warming up by passing the ball around the pitch. The players cannot pass the ball back to the passer and they can't pass the ball to the player immediate to their right or left. How many passes will it take till the starter gets the ball back?

F. 6
G. 5
H. 4
J. 3
K. 2

25. The expression $9x^2(2x^5 - 5x^7)$ is equivalent to:

   A. $18x^{10} - 45x^{14}$

   B. $18x^7 - 45x^9$

   C. $-18x^{10} + 45x^{14}$

   D. $-18x^7 + 45x^9$

   E. $27x^{-4}$

26. $-5|-3 + 9| = ?$

   F. 35

   G. -60

   H. 60

   J. 30

   K. -30

27. In the right triangle $\triangle$CAT below, $\overline{DG} \parallel \overline{CT}$, and $\overline{DG} \perp \overline{CA}$ at B. Line $\overline{AT}$ is 15 units. What is the length of side $\overline{CT}$?

   A. 5

   B. 15

   C. $9\sqrt{2}$

   D. 9

   E. $5\sqrt{2}$

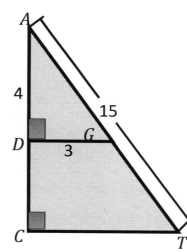

28. A child sleds down a hill at a constant rate. The chart below shows the distance the child sleds in x feet over the interval $t = 0$ seconds to $t = 5$ seconds.

t	0	1	2	3	4	5
x	5	7	9	11	13	15

Which of the following equations represents this data?

   F. $x = t + 5$

   G. $x = 2t + 7$

   H. $x = 2t + 5$

   J. $x = 5t + 2$

   K. $x = 5t + 7$

29. The inequality $5(x + 3) > 6(x - 4)$ is equivalent to which of the following inequalities?

   A. $x < 39$

   B. $x < -39$

   C. $x < 9$

   D. $x < -9$

   E. $x < 7.5$

30. A square has a side length of 5 inches. One vertex lies on (3,1) on a square coordinate grid marked in inches. Which of the following points could also be a vertex of the square?

   F. (0, 2)

   G. (-2, 5)

   H. (8, -3)

   J. (-2, 6)

   K. (5, -3)

31. For ΔLMO, shown below, which of the following is an expression for K in terms of J?

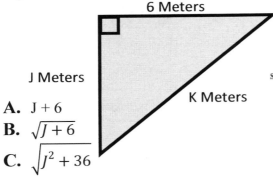

6 Meters

J Meters

K Meters

A. $J + 6$

B. $\sqrt{J + 6}$

C. $\sqrt{J^2 + 36}$

D. $\sqrt{J^2 + 6}$

E. $\sqrt{J^2 - 36}$

32. There are 14 red marbles, 6 blue marbles, and 10 yellow marbles in a bag. How many blue marbles needed to be added to the 30 pre-existing marbles to have a $\frac{2}{5}$ chance of randomly drawing a blue marble?

F. 6
G. 7
H. 8
J. 9
K. 10

33. Which quadrants of the standard (x,y) coordinate plane below contain the equation $6x - 3y = 9$?

quadrants of the standard (x,y) coordinate plane

II   I

III   IV

A. I and II only
B. II and III only
C. I, II, and III only
D. I, III, and IV only
E. II, III, and IV only

34. The graph of $y = -7x^2 + 13$ passes through $(1, 3G)$ in the standard (X, Y) Coordinate. What's the value of G?

F. 1
G. 2
H. 3
J. 4
K. 5

35. John, Jackie, and Jason shared a pizza. John had $\frac{3}{5}$ of the pizza, Jackie had $\frac{3}{10}$ of the pizza and Jason had what was left. What was the ratio John's share to Jackie's share to Jason's share?

A. 6:3:1
B. 3:3:1
C. 3:2:1
D. 3:6:1
E. 6:1:2

36. A circle on a standard (x, y) coordinate plane has an equation of $x^2 + (y-7)^2 = 54$. What is the radius of the circle and what is the center coordinates of the circle?

	Radius	Center
F.	$\sqrt{54}$	(7,0)
G.	54	(7,0)
H.	$\sqrt{54}$	(0,7)
J.	54	(0,7)
K.	27	(0,7)

37. The figure below consists of a square and 2 semicircles. What is the outside perimeter, in centimeters of the shape?

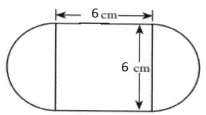

A. $24 + 6\pi$
B. $24 + 12\pi$
C. $12 + 6\pi$
D. $12 + 12\pi$
E. $12 + 24\pi$

38. In the figure below E and B are midpoints of lines $\overline{AG}$ and $\overline{AC}$ respectivly. Lines $\overline{EF}$ and $\overline{AG}$ are $\perp$ at point E. What is the ratio of the shaded area to unshaded?

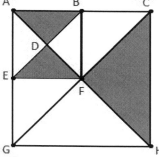

F. 1:3
G. 3:1
H. 5:3
J. 3:5
K. Cannot be determined from the information given

39. The coordinates of the end points of $\overline{LM}$, in the standard coordinate plane (X, Y), are (-3, -5) and (9, 5). What is the x-coordinate of the midpoint of $\overline{LM}$?

A. 1
B. 3
C. 4.5
D. 6
E. 2.5

40. That is the surface area, in square centimeters, of a 7 cm cube?

A. 168
B. 49
C. 196
D. 343
E. 294

41. The equations below are linear equations of a system where g, h and k are positive integers

$$gy - hx = k$$
$$gy + hx = k$$

Which of the following describes the graph of at least one such system of equations in the standard coordinate plane (X,Y)?

I.   2 parallel lines
II. 2 intersecting lines
III. A single line

A. I only
B. II only
C. III only
D. I and II only
E. I, II, and III

42. Based off the below diagram what is the distance between you and the mall?

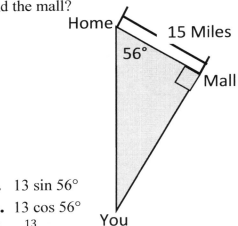

F. 13 sin 56°
G. 13 cos 56°
H. $\frac{13}{\cos 56°}$
J. $\frac{13}{\sin 56°}$
K. 13 tan 56°

43. The circle graph below shows the distribution of kids in each grade. If one student is randomly selected to be interviewed what are the odds (selected grade level: all other grade levels) that the first child selected is in 2nd grade?

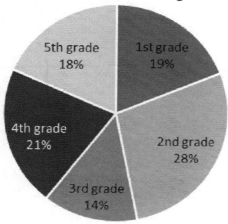

A. 2:5
B. 7:25
C. 7:18
D. 14:30
E. 28:35

Use the following Information to answer questions 44-46

The figure below shows the design of a stain glass window. The 2 squares shown are inscribed in the circle. All triangles are congruent. The vertical center seam is 20 cm long.

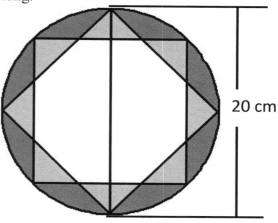

20 cm

44. The stained glass window has how many lines of symmetry?
F. 2
G. 4
H. 7
J. 8
K. Infinitely many

303

45. What is the area of the stained glass window, to the nearest 0.1 square centimeters?

A. 628.3
B. 314.2
C. 1256.6
D. 2513.3
E. 400

46. Dominic has been hired to create a replica of the stained glass window above but with a diameter 20% larger than the original diameter. How long will Dominic need to make the vertical center seam, in centimeters?

F. 2
G. 4
H. 20
J. 24
K. 28

47. In the figure below $\overline{GB} \parallel \overline{HC}$, $\overline{HA}$ bisects $< GH$, and $< BGH$ is 80°. What is the measure of $< GAH$? (Picture is not drawn to scale)

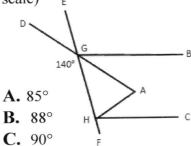

A. 85°
B. 88°
C. 90°
D. 95°
E. Cannot be determined from the given information

48. In the circle below, $\overline{BC}$ and $\overline{AE}$ intersect at F which is the center of the circle. The measure of $< ACB$ is 20°. What is the measure of $< AFB$?

F. 20°
G. 30°
H. 40°
J. 50°
K. 60°

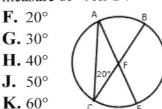

49. What would the value of a need to be for the following system of equations to have an infinite number of solutions?

$$3x - y = 6$$

$$2x - 4y = 2a$$

A. 2
B. 3
C. 6
D. 18
E. 36

Use the following Information to answer questions 50-52

Mackenzie makes short and long necklaces. It takes 1.5 hour to make a short necklace and 2 hours to make a long necklace. In the shaded region below the graph of a system of inequalities represents the weekly constraints Mackenzie faces when making the necklaces. For making s short neclaces and l long neklaces Mackenzie makes a profit of $15s + 20l$ dollars. Mackenzie sells all the necklaces she makes.

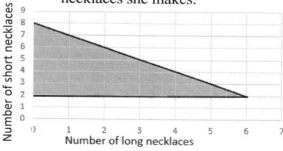

Number of short necklaces

Number of long necklaces

50. The weekly constraints represented by the straight line segment that contains (6,2) means that each week Mackenzie makes at least how many short necklaces?

F. 0
G. 1
H. 2
J. 3
K. 4

305

51. During June for every hour Mackenzie works she donates $2 dollars to local charities. This year she makes 22 short necklaces and 14 long necklaces. What percentage of her profits will she donate?

A. 10%

B. 15%

C. 18%

D. 20%

E. 25%

52. What is the minimum profit Mackenzie will make every week?

F. $0

G. $120

H. $30

J. $20

K. $75

53. The determinate of a matrix $\begin{bmatrix} a & b \\ c & d \end{bmatrix}$ equals $ad - cb$. What must the value of x for the matrix $\begin{bmatrix} 6 & -x \\ x & -2 \end{bmatrix}$ to have a determinant of 15?

A. 2

B. 3

C. -3

D. $2\sqrt{3}$

E. $3\sqrt{3}$

54. Using the formula for investment $A = P(1 + r)^t$. Where A is the total amount after investing P dollars at r rate for t years. What is the amount of p dollars originally invested if the end total is $12,500, the rate is 3% and the money was invested for 5 years?

F. $10,783

G. $3367

H. $10,005

J. $102

K. $1529

55. If x and y are real numbers such that $x < -1$ and $y > 1$ then which of the following inequalities will always be true?

A. $|x| > |y|$

B. $|x|^2 > |y|^2$

C. $\frac{x}{y} > 1$

D. $\frac{y}{3} - 7 > \frac{x}{3} - 7$

E. $x^2 + 5 > y^2 + 5$

56. Triangles ΔRST and ΔXYZ are shown below. The given side lengths are in feet. The area of ΔRST is 45 square feet. What is the area of ΔXYZ, in square feet? Triangles are not drawn to scale.

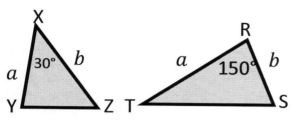

F. 30
G. 40
H. 45
J. 50
K. 60

57. Triangle ΔDFG is shown below. The measure of <D is 60°, $\overline{DF}$ = 17 cm, and $\overline{DG}$ = 21 cm. Which of the following is the value of length $\overline{FG}$, in centimeters?
(Note: For a triangle with side lengths of a, b, and c opposite angles $< A, < B$ and $< C$, respectively, the law of sines states $\frac{sin<A}{a} = \frac{sin<B}{b} = \frac{sin<C}{c}$ and the law of cosines states $c^2 = a^2 + b^2 - 2ab \cos < C$.)

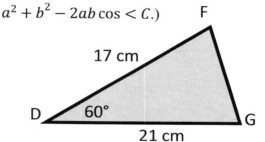

A. $17\sin60°$
B. $21\sin60°$
C. $\sqrt{21^2 + 17^2}$
D. $\sqrt{17^2 - 21^2}$
E. $\sqrt{17^2 + 21^2 - 2(17)(21)\cos 60°}$

58. What is the sum of the first 4 terms of an arithmetic sequence if the first term is zero and the sixth term is 7.5?
F. 15
G. 9
H. 4.5
J. 8
K. 6

59. In the equation $x^2 + mx + n = 0$, when $m = 10$ and $n = 25$ what is x?

A. -5
B. 5
C. -2
D. 2
E. -4

60. The solution of which of the following equations is the set of real numbers that at 14 units from -25?

F. $|x + 14| = 25$
G. $|x - 14| = 25$
H. $|x - 14| = -25$
J. $|x + 25| = 14$
K. $|x - 25| = 14$

Do not go on
until you are out of time

This page intentionally left blank

Practice Test 2: Post Test Key

1.	A	37.	C
2.	J	38.	J
3.	E	39.	B
4.	J	40.	E
5.	C	41.	B
6.	G	42.	K
7.	A	43.	C
8.	F	44.	J
9.	D	45.	B
10.	H	46.	J
11.	E	47.	C
12.	J	48.	H
13.	B	49.	B
14.	K	50.	H
15.	D	51.	D
16.	H	52.	H
17.	A	53.	E
18.	K	54.	F
19.	B	55.	D
20.	J	56.	H
21.	E	57.	E
22.	F	58.	G
23.	C	59.	A
24.	G	60.	K
25.	B		
26.	K		
27.	D		
28.	H		
29.	A		
30.	J		
31.	C		
32.	K		
33.	D		
34.	G		
35.	A		
36.	H		

Scoring Guide

ACT® Score	Raw Score
36	59 – 60
35	57 – 58
34	55 – 56
33	54
32	53
31	52
30	50 – 51
29	49
28	47 – 48
27	45 – 46
26	43 – 44
25	41 – 42
24	38 – 40
23	36 – 37
22	34 – 35
21	33
20	31 – 32
19	29 – 30
18	27 – 28
17	24 – 26
16	19 – 23
15	15 – 18
14	12 – 14
13	10 - 11
12	8 – 9
11	6 – 7
10	5
9	4
8	–
7	3
6	–
5	2
4	–
3	1
2	–
1	0

SELF-ASSESSMENT ZONE			
Raw Score		ACT® Score	

How was your time management?

Asses yourself	I did ok	I was a little challenged	I was very challenged
Long word problems	☐	☐	☐
Trigonometry problems	☐	☐	☐
Basic Algebra Problems	☐	☐	☐
Geometry Problems	☐	☐	☐
Fraction Problems	☐	☐	☐
Parentage Problems	☐	☐	☐

What do you think is going well so far?

What do you need to do in order to improve?

This page intentionally left blank

NOTES AND REMINDERS

NOTES AND REMINDERS

NOTES AND REMINDERS

27738410R00181

Made in the USA
Lexington, KY
07 January 2019